PROFESSIONAL WRITING

The Professional Practices in Adult Education and Human Resource Development Series explores issues and concerns of practitioners who work in the broad range of settings in adult and continuing education and human resource development.

The books are intended to provide information and strategies on how to make practice more effective for professionals and those they serve. They are written from a practical viewpoint and provide a forum for instructors, administrators, policy makers, counselors, trainers, managers, program and organizational developers, instructional designers, and other related professionals.

Editorial correspondence should be sent to the Editor-in-Chief:

Michael W. Galbraith
Florida Atlantic University
Department of Educational Leadership
College of Education
Boca Raton, FL 33431

DATE DUE

SEP 2 9 1994		
OCT 0 3 1994		

DEMCO 38-297

PROFESSIONAL WRITING

Processes, Strategies, and Tips for Publishing in Educational Journals

Roger Hiemstra
Professor
Instructional Design and Adult Learning
Syracuse University
and Professional Writing Consultant

and

Ellen M. Brier
Adjunct Professor
Department of Educational Leadership
Department of Human and Organizational Development
Vanderbilt University

KRIEGER PUBLISHING COMPANY
MALABAR, FLORIDA
1994

Original Edition 1994

Printed and Published by
KRIEGER PUBLISHING COMPANY
KRIEGER DRIVE
MALABAR, FLORIDA 32950

Copyright © 1994 by Roger Hiemstra and Ellen M. Brier

Library of Congress Cataloging-In-Publication Data

Hiemstra, Roger.
    Professional writing : processes, strategies, and tips for
publishing in educational journals / Roger Hiemstra and Ellen M.
Brier.
      p. cm.
    Includes bibliographical references and index.
    ISBN 0-89464-660-5 (acid-free paper). — ISBN 0-89464-806-3 (pbk.)
    1. Authorship. 2. Education—Scholarship. 3. Scholarly
periodicals.   I. Brier, Ellen M. II. Title.
PN146.H39   1993
808'.02—dc20   93-7439
                                       CIP

10 9 8 7 6 5 4 3 2

CONTENTS

PREFACE

Writing and publishing can be a gratifying professional experience. When you write and publish your first article not only do you experience an immense feeling of pride and enjoyment, you also join the ranks of many others who successfully communicate in writing with colleagues. Such professionals include teachers, administrators, higher education faculty, health and human service employees, trainers in business and industry, independent researchers, and students studying a profession. These people carry out various educational tasks, all of which can be enhanced through professional publications.

For most people the process of writing and successfully publishing articles involves hard work, patience, an inquisitive mind, the willingness to accept both criticism and rejection, and, perhaps most important of all, perseverance. As a prospective author you need to understand some things about this writing process and corresponding publishing elements.

Professional Writing: Processes, Strategies, and Tips for Publishing in Educational Journals provides a close look at how writing and publishing educational articles works. The book emanates from the authors' combined teaching, writing, publishing, and editing experiences of more than 40 years. It is a practical guide for writers, filled with insights, discussions, tips, strategies, and recommendations for enhancing writing skills.

We have set four goals for *Professional Writing*:

1. To provide you with information, tips, and strategies on how to write effectively for educational periodicals.

2. To talk about professional writing and publishing from a very practical viewpoint.

3. To write in a clear, jargon-free, and friendly style so that the book is readable, interesting, and useful.

4. To discuss the assessment of text from the perspectives of the reader, the reviewer, and you, the writer.

A number of books offer some assistance on professional writing and publishing, but this volume provides information on what editors are looking for, strategies you should know to quickly improve each draft you write, and processes you can use to remove writing blocks or maximize the usefulness of resources readily available to you. You will learn how to organize thoughts and information, determine what a journal expects, and ensure your article is meeting all stylistic requirements.

If you want to improve your writing skills, this book also helps you identify, understand, and work through necessary stages of the writing and publication process from prewriting exercises through submission of a manuscript to an editor or publisher. It provides specific steps we believe you should take as you move an article from conception to a finished product. Throughout the book we provide tables, figures, and highlighted points to facilitate your remembering the essential ideas.

The book is intended to serve as a guide for understanding and improving personal writing styles, increasing writing productivity, and refining professional discourse. It provides you with new tips and ideas for using personal computers in your writing efforts.

Finally, the book serves as a resource on some essential writing "how to's," as well as on publication possibilities and review strategies. The chapters are designed and organized to address your questions, concerns, and interests as a writer or prospective writer. At the end of each chapter we suggest some exercises designed to help you understand and build on your current expertise. It is our expectation that you will turn time and time again to the book for new insights into or reminders of what is needed for publishing successfully.

We conclude this preface with the same message we use to end our writing workshops. We can provide only a matrix of ideas and approaches, from which you must extract, synthesize, and adapt those aspects that fit your particular writing needs and approaches. In all of this we wish you much success and encourage you to continue your writing efforts.

ACKNOWLEDGMENTS

Writing is no less a social act as it is a solitary one. As such it is fitting to recognize those individuals and groups who have contributed to the development of this book.

There are numerous learners who have responded to our efforts to share experiences and ideas about the publishing process. Our heartfelt thanks for their feedback and many efforts to improve their writing. To those with publishing success we feel real pride and hope we helped in various ways.

We also have some personal thanks to those who helped us become interested in the writing process. This book could not have been written without the support, encouragement, and patience of family, friends, and colleagues.

Roger thanks his wife, Janet, who helped him as a beginning professional struggle to improve his writing. Her critiques, feedback, and editing suggestions were and remain very important. He also has watched with amazement as his two children, Nancy and David, have grown into young adults with tremendous abilities to express themselves through the written word.

Ellen wishes to recognize those who taught and encouraged her to write, the first among whom was Robert T. Brier, Sr., her father. Also, many students and colleagues have contributed to this text, often in ways unknown to them. Worthy of special mention is her colleague and husband, John M. Braxton, and her colleague Diane Cooke. Finally, her inspiring sons, Colin and Sean, gave her the energy to get the text completed.

THE AUTHORS

Roger Hiemstra is professor of instructional design and adult learning at Syracuse University. He received his B.S. degree in agricultural economics from Michigan State University in 1964, his M.S. degree in extension education from Iowa State University in 1967, and his Ph.D. degree in adult community education from the University of Michigan in 1970. He was a Mott Intern in the community education program in Flint, Michigan, for a year during his doctoral degree work.

Hiemstra served from 1964 to 1967 as a county extension agent for the Iowa Extension Service, starting his professional writing through regular newsletters and technical reports. From 1970 to 1976 he taught adult education at the University of Nebraska where he first encountered the publish or perish syndrome and published two books and several journal articles.

He served as professor and department chair of adult education at Iowa State University from 1976 to 1980. During this period he was involved in one more book project, published several journal articles and monographs, and began teaching writing workshops to graduate students.

Since 1980 he has served as professor and chair of adult education at Syracuse University. He has been involved with four book projects, written numerous book chapters and journal articles, and served as the editor of two national journals. He continues to teach writing workshops to graduate students and others and has helped a number of people in their initial publishing efforts.

Ellen M. Brier has taught and studied writing for almost two decades. She holds a B.A. magna cum laude and a M.A.

from the State University of New York at Albany. In addition, she has a M.Ed. and an Ed.D. in higher education administration and history from Columbia University where she had a Michael Brick Fellowship.

Brier has developed and taught numerous writing courses and workshops in college and university settings as well as in health care organizations. She has worked with university faculty members to help them increase their publication productivity and develop their writing skills. She has addressed professional organizations on the important role of writers in professional practice. Further, she has conducted numerous seminars and workshops on understanding and overcoming writing blocks. She also has offered graduate courses on professional writing.

Along with teaching writing, she has published numerous articles, co-authored a chapter in *Advances in Writing, Volume II: Writing In Academic Disciplines*, reviewed books, and reviewed articles for several journals. She frequently has served as a consultant on writing.

Currently she is an adjunct professor in the Department of Educational Leadership and Human and Organizational Development of Vanderbilt University, Nashville, Tennessee. She also serves as an educational consultant.

CHAPTER 1

Writing for Publication in Educational Journals

"Mommy, is it true that reading can take you anywhere?" a curious four-year old asked.

"Of course," his mother quickly responded. "Reading can transport you to all kinds of exciting and wonderful places. It can blast you to outer space and carry you across oceans to faraway places! It can bring you inside of your own mind. Reading is a super vehicle."

"Well, Mommy, if reading can take you anywhere, how do we get back home?"

After reflecting on the profound and insightful nature of this preschooler's question, the mother attempted to calm the boy's fear of reading's power and excite him about reading's possibilities. Writing is analogous to reading. It can take you anywhere and it can return you home. It is a powerful vehicle. But its power can produce anxiety for the uninitiated considering participating.

The decision to become a writer can be frightening. The force can arrest even the confident. Writing revolves around taking a chance intellectually, whether you are approaching writing an article for the first time or an experienced professional facing the prospect of starting a new book project.

Even though writing for publication is risky, it is also very rewarding. The prospect of having your written work criticized or rejected can prove intimidating but the satisfaction from seeing your ideas in print can be very high. Placing your writing in the public arena for other professionals to examine takes courage. You need to be committed to your own ideas, experience, knowledge, and skills. Faith in what you have to say to others is an essential ingredient for writing for publication and it can return many joys.

Publishing an article is not the result of mysterious forces or good luck. It does not happen because you as a writer will it or win it. It does happen because you want to write. Producing a publishable article is also the product of hard work. It will not always even be enjoyable work, but it most likely will be satisfying work. You can do it and do it successfully!

WHY SHOULD YOU WRITE?

Writing can provide you with lots of personal and professional satisfaction and occasionally some fun! Writing and getting your work published usually generates excitement. It is gratifying to transfer your ideas, observations, experience, knowledge, or inquiry into written text. Let's briefly look at some reasons you as a professional should consider developing a manuscript.

Writing and the Profession

In the process of writing you not only communicate with yourself and your audience but you also learn about your profession. The writing process itself is instructive. It can produce insights and new knowledge for the writer.

Writing for publication also is a superb way to inform and be informed by your profession:

- You can influence your field as well as advance it.
- You can improve your writing and communication skills.
- Practice and scholarship can be enhanced.
- You can be a part of connecting practice and theory.
- You can disseminate new ideas, techniques, theories, and research findings.
- Widely held, traditional, or evolving beliefs can be challenged.

In addition to advancing and informing your field, you can advance your own career and simultaneously develop as a professional. Colleges, universities, and many other organizations reward employees who successfully publish. Speaking and job opportunities may even occur with publishing success. The role writing plays in the professions is explored in Chapter 2.

The Writer

Unfortunately, for many professionals in education, health, the social services, and other areas interested in communicating with colleagues, their own educational backgrounds and training have not provided much preparation in writing. Thus, a strong need exists to learn the "what" and "how" of writing for journal publication. Fortunately, writing is not a mystical art; you can learn about publishing strategies and develop your writing skills.

In Chapter 3 we discuss defining and empowering yourself as a writer. Before you begin to generate text you need to view yourself as a writer. You need to recognize the skill, knowledge, experience, and perspective you bring to the task of writing. You need to identify your strengths as well as the requirements of the task. You need to approach your writing with a clear sense of yourself as a writer and a "I can do, I will do" attitude or spirit.

The Writing Process

For many writers, effective and productive writing involves four stages. Each stage is not necessary every time you develop an article nor are the stages always sequential and discrete. However, successful authors usually employ several text development techniques in moving their ideas and eventual written products through the stages of development.

There are four stages to a successful writing process: Prewriting, text developing, revising, and editing. Throughout the book we refer to these four stages. Other authors may use different labels for these stages, or they may conceptualize the associated steps differently. One distinction of our discussion is that we differentiate between revising and editing. In so doing we present them as distinct stages rather than editing being a part of revising. However, you may find it necessary to work simultaneously on more than one segment of the writing process. An important key to mastering both writing and publishing is competent management of all stages.

Prewriting marks the beginning of the writing process. It is filled with activities that produce ideas, terms, phrases, organizational and syntactical patterns, questions, outlines, and lists. Prewriting thus includes a wide range of generative activity, much of which leads eventually to the development of text. Chapters 4 and 8 present and discuss many prewriting techniques aimed at facilitating your writing confidence and productivity. Through prewriting you position yourself to write. You prepare the intellectual ground for producing text.

Text developing, a stage often considered to be writing, is not ordinarily the initial stage in the process. Unfortunately, for many frustrated writers, writing prematurely begins with attempts at text development rather than prewriting. Text developing should result in a manuscript draft that emerges from various prewriting activities, considerable intellectual stimulation, and plain old hard work.

The stages of revising and editing are often confused or misunderstood, too. Revising text or part of a text means literally seeing it again, to rethink it. This is not simply correcting a grammatical error or improving an awkward construction or phrase. Revision entails a new way of viewing the text. Editing simply means polishing the text. Between these two stages exists a substantive difference. In Chapter 4 we discuss revising and editing more fully.

The Text

In Chapter 5 we examine text as a product of the writing process. This discussion focuses on content, structure, perspective, and the technicalities, rules, and conventions of style. It provides you with a way of relating to the text and a way of viewing textual relationships, particularly in terms of audience, purpose, and use.

Writing Blocks

Obstacles of various sorts are an intrinsic part of the writing process. In Chapter 6 we focus on writing blocks. We discuss types of blocks, the debilitating role they can play in the writing process, and some strategies for successfully working through them. This chapter serves as a bridge between the writing process and the publishing process.

The Publication Process

Writing for publication does not end with completing a polished article. Getting the article published represents another important process. This process is quite distinct from the writing process. However, they share one thing in common. Success involves careful management of the various components.

You may wonder how you can successfully publish when you know many articles are rejected. Focus on the positive, as many articles are published. Success is not a matter of luck or personal and professional politics. Successfully publishing an article depends in part on your writing competent text and finding the correct publication fit. Your article's best placement in the publication arena gives it the highest probability of acceptance.

Chapters 7 and 8 provide information on preparing and submitting manuscripts. Here we look at the publication process from both an author's and an editor's perspective, perspectives based on our own writing and editorial experiences.

Chapter 9 also provides information of value to the publication process by giving tips and ideas on how to maximize the personal computer in your writing efforts. The last chapter of the book, 10, provides some special ideas, strategies, and issues to consider in producing successful writing.

As a published or aspiring author, you may be interested in knowing some common reasons articles are rejected so that you might avoid these pitfalls. You may like to know typical suggestions editors make about revising articles for reconsideration.

Table 1.1 presents rejection reasons and rewrite suggestions for two adult education publications. In essence, editors are looking for articles that will be read. They may look for manuscripts fitting an upcoming issue's theme or a category of articles published in most issues. They may be looking for a manuscript on the cutting edge of knowledge or one that is somewhat controversial. Above all, most editors are looking for articles that are well written and that communicate clearly to readers.

CHARACTERISTICS OF SUCCESSFUL WRITERS

As a professional, you are capable of publishing successfully in educational periodicals. You might want to start with an essay response in reaction to an article published in a particular journal, a book review aimed for a professional magazine, or a report of a local program's special continuing education feature you submit to the ERIC data base. You may feel ready to submit an article that describes a research project or one on some ideas you have for needed educational programs or policy.

What are some characteristics that differentiate successful from unsuccessful writers? Perhaps most important are commitment, self-discipline, and perseverance. To write a publishable article it must be written! This statement may seem self-evident, but we have seen too many of our colleagues continuously in the process of writing "that article" which somehow never gets finished and sometimes never even gets started.

Getting "it" written may entail developing a schedule where your writing is rigorously routinized several times each week. It may involve making time for the writing process in

Table 1.1. Article Rejection Reasons and Rewrite Suggestions

REJECTION REASONS	LL:AY [a]	AEQ [b]
Inappropriate for the magazine or journal	31%	12%
Poorly written	26%	15%
Not written at the level of most readers	13%	10%
Article contains no new information	8%	6%
Unacceptable form or style	6%	12%
Too anecdotal or localized in interest	6%	2%
Not well supported by literature or theory	5%	20%
Unacceptable length	5%	8%
Unacceptable methodology	0%	15%
REWRITE SUGGESTIONS	**LL:AY**	**AEQ**
Improve or polish writing	37%	25%
Strengthen tie to adult education	18%	5%
Shorten the article	15%	12%
Provide a stronger ending	12%	8%
Provide closer adherence to stylistic guides	10%	28%
Provide a better explanation of methodology	8%	12%
Provide a better review of relevant literature	0%	10%

[a] *Lifelong Learning: The Adult Years* for the period of 1980–1983. During this time 199 refereed articles were published, 172 were rejected, and 144 were sent back for rewriting (some of which were later accepted).

[b] *Adult Education Quarterly* for the period of 1986–1989. During this time 58 refereed articles were published, 231 were rejected, and 88 were sent back for rewriting (some of which were later accepted).

lieu of some other activity. It may require you to reprioritize what is important. Continuing to work diligently on a writing project until it is finished certainly will be required. It may even mean that you must use various strategies to overcome writing blocks if they are encountered along the way. We describe several such strategies in Chapter 6.

Curiosity and a love of lifelong learning also are fundamental to success. You may ask why a particular program in higher education worked or failed. You might want to understand more about learning theory in order to provide new information to colleagues. You may wish to tell others why your particular instructional design effort seemed to be so effective. You might want to carry out an experimental research project on what techniques work best for teaching physicians a medical procedure and then report the results in a scholarly journal.

In addition to commitment, self-discipline, perseverance, curiosity, and the love of lifelong learning, productive, successful writers need to be open to criticism. Indeed, a wise writer seeks the critique and honest feedback of others. Although you may find criticism painful and frightening at first, it is well worth the risk because through the critiquing process your text stands to improve and you stand to develop as a writer.

If you want to be a writer you have to take chances, you must be willing to try, and you need to experiment with ideas, words, and structures. Finally you need to define yourself as a writer when you write and take on that role in a serious manner.

WRITING RESOURCES

As a writer you need a variety of writing resources. Perhaps most important are the stylistic guidelines from those journals you target for your articles. Most periodicals publish condensed versions of their stylistic requirements in each issue, usually near the front or back cover. Occasionally some periodicals publish an extended version that details all their stylistic requirements, or you may need to contact the editor for such information. If it is difficult to obtain such information, in Chapter 7 we detail a procedure for developing your own stylistic guidelines for any periodical.

A successful writer acquires and uses a variety of writing resources. You will want various reference materials such as a dictionary, thesaurus, book of quotations, informational almanac, and writer's handbook. Books on writing fiction may provide occasional assistance if you wish to build a vignette or use a case study to illustrate a certain idea. One or more generic books on style and usage also will be helpful. We recommend

Strunk and White's (1979) classic work, *The Elements of Style*, for concise and clear advice on good writing.

As we detail in Chapter 9, there is a growing list of computer software programs to support the educational author. Word processing software is widely available for almost any type of computer. Many of these programs contain helpful features such as spell checking, outlining, and index building. Many specialized software packages exist to assist with the writing process. These packages include grammar checking programs, readability scale calculators, and data management software. Some word processing packages contain additional aids, such as a thesaurus, dictionary, macro building capability, and desktop publishing feature. Software also is available to facilitate data analysis for both quantitative and qualitative research-based articles.

The computer provides you as a writer with tremendous power to increase your writing productivity as well as the quality of your text. In saving you time, it can multiply your ability to develop refined text. In essence, the computer is an exciting writing resource that can empower you as a writer.

Empowerment, improvement, and development are constant themes throughout this book. Our goal is to assist you on the way to becoming a published author. You possess all the ingredients. It is simply a case of finding the right mix and context so that you can write successfully. Why deny your professional colleagues the opportunity to learn from you? Your field needs you and your written contributions for its continued growth and development. Be an active participant and join with us in examining the processes of writing and publishing.

EXERCISES

1. Compile two lists of information. One would include reasons why you want to have your writing published. Use personal brainstorming, talking with colleagues, or any introspective technique that works. No reason should be discounted or discarded. You may need to work on this list for several

days. When it seems complete, go back through and priori-
tize the items. Use this list as your personal disciplining tool
whenever you begin writing. The second list is a compilation
of topics about which you wish to write. You may even want
to keep an idea file in which you place writing ideas as they
come to you. This list will continue to supply you with writing ideas as it grows and evolves over time.

2. Check your personal library for writing resources you may
   already possess, such as a dictionary, thesaurus, stylistic
   guide book, and books of quotes. Bring them all together
   in one handy location and begin to add some of the sources
   noted in this book and others that you locate. Think, too,
   of computer software that you can add to your personal
   collection of writing resources.

CHAPTER 2

Writing and the Professions

Writing plays a leading role in all professions. Unlike the spoken word whose nature is fleeting, the written word endures. Its life goes far beyond the moment. It is written by virtue of being contained in a text, a document. The written word can be read repeatedly and not be changed by different readers. Although various readers may interpret a text differently, text is what it is. It cannot change unless revised by the writer.

Through written professional discourse, both the professions and the professionals in them are served. Without development of a substantial body of written discourse, particularly published text books and journal articles, a field could not attain recognition as a profession. Further, in order to obtain professional status a field must generate, control, and refine its own knowledge base. Professions exercise these prerogatives in their writings, particularly their publications.

Throughout this chapter, we examine the ways writing functions in a profession. In addition, we identify reasons for contributing to your field's body of literature and the role you can play. Finally, we consider both personal and professional benefits of writing for your profession.

FUNCTIONS OF WRITING

Let's begin by exploring the functions of writing in a profession. On a most fundamental level, a profession formally communicates through its writings. In written discourse, especially through publications, a field speaks to itself, its members, and those interested in the field.

Professional journals serve the widest range of readers, and typically reach the largest audiences. Thus, along with books, journal articles are primary communication vehicles. They act as forums for professional discussion. Try to imagine a field without professional journals. The prospect is unimaginable.

A major information source for you as a professional is professional writings in the field and in related fields. Through reading textbooks and journals about happenings, trends, issues, discoveries, new techniques, practices, and policies you keep in touch with other practitioners and scholars across your profession. By participating in a field's published written discourse, you are part of a communication well beyond the local context of your work.

This participation, even as a reader of the published works, can enlarge your communication network to include an entire professional association, a region, a state, the nation, the world. Professional writings exponentially enlarge the communication possibilities by expanding your professional context as well as contacts. Whether you interact as a reader, writer, or both reader and writer, your professional self benefits from exposure to the works of authors in and about your field. The communication function of professional writing also affects all members of your profession. In essence, professional writing can be powerful in its impact on individuals and consequently on groups.

SERVING A PROFESSION

Let's look more closely at ways professional writing serves a profession and its members. A field's history in part rests with its writings both through primary and secondary sources. With journal articles you can gain insight into your field's who, what, why, and when. Professional writing plays a critical and essential part in the transmission of a profession's history. It also serves as a tool to inform or guide current practice and future development. Although history is ultimately interpretative, by examining written discourse you can determine relevant facts.

Related to serving historical purposes, professional writings work to establish, maintain, and advance a profession. Quite literally, the profession is composed in writing. By subjecting itself to written exploration, particularly in journal articles and conference papers, a profession creates, nurtures, and promotes itself among members and other professions. Writing functions as a forum for self-definition, growth, and development.

Professional writing affords the opportunity for elaborated self-exploration. Through writings a profession puts itself under the lens of an intellectual microscope, the eyes of members and interested readers. Such readers possess different perspectives and attitudes toward the profession under examination. By using individual and collective responses to this continuous examination, a profession expands and refines ways of defining itself, manipulates and adjusts boundaries, alters practices, and assesses values, perspectives, and postures. In so doing it acquires and projects a clearer, more carefully delineated professional image.

A profession sustains itself through writings. It systematically incorporates contributions to the field and fosters professional growth. In written discourse, a profession encourages and chides itself. It reflects on progress and achievement as well as failure. It tests new possibilities and affirms or rejects existing measures, ideas, and theories. Through active written discourse a profession keeps itself alive and lively. You can be a part of such vigor with your writing.

Further, a profession advances itself by promoting new concepts, proposing new practices or refinements of existing ones, and making recommendations for change. Professional writings act as a speculative arena for innovation, invention, and initiation. A profession's future is entertained, encouraged, and ensured in its writings. A profession which ceases writing about and for itself is an endangered, if not extinct species.

Evaluation of a profession occurs in its writings, too. This evaluative role constitutes a significant dimension of quality control in a profession. Frequently in their writings, scholars and practitioners judge the quality of a field's life. They judge research and application, policy and practice. Professional assessment is an essential ingredient for establishing, enacting, or refining standards, as well as considering new quality measures.

THE EDUCATIONAL ROLE
OF PROFESSIONAL WRITING

Published materials serve students and professionals alike. Professional writings always have an educational function. They are used by students and faculty in instructional contexts. In addition, as part of their on-going professional development, practicing professionals rely on written works. In order to keep current and learn what is professionally new and different, you must be a regular consumer of professional writings. Such writings initiate students into the realm of theory and practice. They facilitate and stimulate development of the practicing professional. They serve as a path to increased knowledge, skills, and understandings.

Through published writings, a profession's knowledge base, those theories, understandings, and insights peculiar to or used by the field, are expanded, advanced, and controlled. The extent to which a profession controls its own knowledge base determines its professional autonomy. Contributions to knowledge, skill, and practice gain professional attention and recognition via written discourse. The accumulation of written contributions promotes advancement and stimulates a field's progressive development. Theory can enter the world of practice by way of the written text. Skill and practice also are served by writing.

In its written discourse a profession has a forum for discussion, dialogue, and debate. Ideas, practices, and policies generate enthusiastic and energetic discourse, ranging from friendly to hostile. The written arena provides a structured, formal opportunity to consider and debate differing views. Writing can work as a stage for enacting professional controversies and facilitating systematic dialogue about various professional issues.

THE ROLE YOU CAN PLAY

The role of writing in any profession is unique. Its potential is limited only by the capabilities of those professionals who write. Scholar or practitioner, writers through published work contribute significantly to their professions. Writing creates opportunities for not only significant contribution but also professional recognition and advancement. You can invest in your profession and enhance a relationship with the profession by writing.

As you consider writing within the context of your field, think about the many roles your writing can play. You possess a unique set of professional experiences. Learn to use them to your own and your field's advantage. Individual experience always is invested with a common worth. This value has professional applicability.

In order to contribute to a profession, your individual experiences need to find written expression. The range of experience open to written exploration is limitless. You can write about a particular practice you deem successful or effective, a refinement or modification of skills that works, an intriguing or illustrative case or client. You might want to discuss the details of a program or the pitfalls of a procedure. You might reflect on an experience and thereby provide an instrument for gaining insight. However you view your experience, you can put it to work for your professional community by writing about it in an article.

In addition to sharing personal experiences, you can share your ideas, unique insights, understanding, and perspectives. Write about what you think, believe, and value. Develop your professional perspectives and philosophy into a written text. Enter professional dialogues and debates by logically developing your own point of view. Refine this outlook in a written article. Use the text in your article as a vehicle for learning and thereby refine your own thinking while influencing or at least stimulating the thoughts of others.

Review the writings of others. By writing an integrative or evaluative article, you can present a different and new set of insights into the works of other authors. In doing so, you are contributing to the profession.

Of course, you can contribute to the field's discourse by writing about studies you have conducted. Traditional or innovative research is always a rich and important source for professionals who want to contribute to the professional literature. Such literature can inform practice and practice can inform future research and theory. Even anecdotal studies provide enriching sources for professional writing.

By writing for your profession you also hold a position of influence. When you write for your colleagues, you call attention to yourself. You create an occasion for professional recognition. Simultaneously you contribute to the recognition and status of your field which is frequently judged by its written discourse. Both you as a writer and your profession as the generic object of your writing stand to benefit if the text, your article, is considered of value. The benefits of positive recognition are clear and closely relate to advancement.

On a personal level, the benefits of professional writing reside in the inherent sense of satisfaction and achievement which come from producing an article for publication. In the process, you learn and grow as a professional. Further, you can gain increased self-confidence and develop professionally enriching relationships with colleagues.

Finally, you can create professional opportunities for yourself. You stand to gain a great deal by writing. The benefits far outweigh the risks. In writing you project a professional self to your field. Take advantage of the many possibilities writing articles offers you. Enjoy the risks and embrace the challenges. Most certainly you have something to write about, so write it!

EXERCISES

1. Think about the various ways you can advance your professional knowledge by engaging in the writing process.
   Reviewing literature, conducting original research, and critiquing the writing of others are some of these. List several
   more that come to mind.

2. Consider the role you would like to play as an author in
   contributing to your profession. This might mean developing
   conceptual models or formulating new theory. It might mean
   specializing in the development of educational policy. Perhaps you will want to play more than one role. Determine
   one or more roles and build a scholarship agenda covering
   several years.

CHAPTER 3

The Writer

The writer provides the thinking and feeling, the brain and heart of writing, both process and product. Further, the writer infuses both this process and text with spirit, soul, and a unique and intangible life source.

Along with thought, feeling, and spirit, the writer also brings vision. The writer's way of seeing externally the outside world and internally the world within incorporates itself into the process and thereby the text. In essence, a writer is both central and essential to writing. To discuss the writing process and any text without discussing the writer would be less than thorough.

In this chapter, our focus is on the writer as writer. First, we examine the concept of a self-defined writer, some popular myths about what it means to be a writer, and the types of writing you can do. We then explore the writer as decision-maker. We look at the writer as critic. Finally, we suggest some characteristics of effective and productive writers.

THE SELF-DEFINED WRITER

To be an effective and productive writer you need a solid, well-defined sense of yourself. You must view yourself in the company of other writers. You should visualize yourself actually writing. At this point, you might be thinking "How can I see myself as a writer if I have never written an article before?" Maybe you are wondering how you could place yourself among writers when you have no experience publishing. Keep in mind, publishing and writing are distinct processes. Publication follows writing.

Publishing is not the necessary consequence of writing, however. Writing for publication is only one of numerous writing purposes. Your goal to write a publishable article for an educational journal is central to the intent of this book. For our discussion of defining yourself as a writer, it is sufficient to point out that you need not be a well-published, award-winning author to consider yourself a writer.

Another commonly held misconception about being a writer purports that specific training or education in the discipline of writing is required. Although some instruction in writing, either self-directed or instructor-directed, can be beneficial to you, it is neither required nor essential. Formal writing instruction does not make a writer. It can contribute to your becoming a writer but only you can make yourself a writer; only you can create a working definition of yourself as a writer.

In addition to the popularly held beliefs that publishing and instruction can bestow the title "writer," another prevalent myth suggests that writers are a class of gifted, highly creative geniuses who live in big cities, artists' communities, or as hermits in commune with nature. These stereotypes of writers generally are incorrect, especially in terms of journal article authors. Talent can be developed and creativity fostered. Both are highly individualistic attributes and express themselves in a variety of ways. Writers represent a variegated pattern of talent and creativity; they can be found in a wide range of living and work contexts.

Another common myth identifies writers only as those individuals who write for a living, those whose income is generated by the act of writing. In other words, according to this belief set, the only real writers are writers by occupation, for example, journalists, technical writers, and possibly editors.

If you believe any of these myths, you need to let go. These beliefs will not serve you in positive ways. They will not contribute to your developing a definition of self as writer. They may even detract from your personal growth and development.

You cannot afford to hold debilitating concepts about the meaning of being a writer.

A writer writes, and anyone who writes is a writer. It is as simple as that. In addition to professional authors who write for a living, scholars and practitioners write, too. Recently, the number of practitioners involved with writing has increased. Along with this increase in writer-practitioners, the volume of practice-based texts has grown. This growth points to a real opportunity for you to write and get published.

First, however, you must see yourself in the writer's role. In building a definition of self as a writer, start by identifying the kinds of writing you typically do and your motivations for doing them. You probably write informal as well as formal material, and you write for personal as well as professional reasons. After identifying such writing activities, you may find you write more than previously thought.

On a personal level you might write letters, lists of things to do, notes, or directions. Perhaps you keep a journal, log, or diary. You may even write poetry, fiction, or songs. Often within the context of daily living you write. Learn to view these exercises in writing as valuable practice. Recognize that you already write and that it has worth. Writing, although personal and informal, is nevertheless real writing. If you produce any kind of written text, you are a writer.

In addition to writing for personal reasons, you also write for work and professional purposes. Think of all the work and profession related writing you do. Work related writing occurs within or for the employing organization. For example, when you write a departmental report or an interoffice memo, you are engaging in professional writing.

Writing for or about a profession can also serve you in writing articles. The audience for your profession related writing is the community of professional colleagues and interested readers you address. Some of these may be in your work setting but others will be outside it. Those readers outside your area of work form the larger group interested in your professional perspective.

Personal	Workplace	Profession Related
diary	abstracts	abstracts
directions	agenda	agenda
journal	charts	articles
letters	directions	books
lists	evaluations	chapters
log	letters	conference papers
notes	lists	directions
	memoranda	editorials
	minutes	letters
	newsletters	memoranda
	notes	minutes
	performance reviews	newsletters
	proposals	notes
	reviews	proposals
	studies	

Figure 3.1 Common genre by category.

When you speak as a professional to whatever audience interested in your topic, you are sharing information for professional purposes. When you write for a professional association's newsletter, when you prepare a syllabus, or when you plan for a workshop you are engaged in professional writing.

We have included some common examples of writing in three categories: personal, workplace, and profession (see Figure 3.1). Some genre or types of writing occur in all three categories. No doubt, you can identify a number of the genre you have experienced writing. In other words, you already are a writer. Start using this self-knowledge to shape, develop, and expand your self-definition in terms of writing.

THE WRITER AS DECISION-MAKER

Many individuals who assume writing tasks for work or professional reasons feel like victims. They have a sense of being held hostage by the need to write. They view themselves this way because writing is seen as something painful done to them rather than something they do and over which they exercise a great deal of control. In Chapter 4, we discuss in great detail how you can manage the overall process and gain back a sense of control.

As you approach writing your article, take charge. Make it happen! Let's look at some of the decisions you will face as you write your article. While the nuts and bolts of the writer as decision-maker are highly peculiar to the actual situation, several broad areas are identifiable.

Let's start by looking at you. Begin by being realistic in your expectations of self. Assess your needs in relation to the task and make some appropriate decisions. For example, how much rest, exercise, and recreation do you need to facilitate your enacting the role of writer? How much social contact would it take to support you as you write? Once you have determined your personal needs, try to accommodate them.

Be systematic in deciding what to do. Develop a standard or regularized approach to your article writing. Organize yourself and attend to details of the process. As a writer, be disciplined, purposeful, and committed to the work of writing.

The higher the quality of your decisions, the greater the quality of your writing. Every aspect of your writing an article for publication is governed by such decisions. Growth in your consciousness of these decisions can increase your effectiveness as a writer. You can also add to your sense of control over the process and the text by making sound decisions.

Authorship is among the first writing decisions you make, and it is usually done early in the process. Will you write your article alone or will you collaborate? There will be many occasions when you will want or need to write by yourself. This book provides you with considerable help for solitary writing.

On the other hand, collaboration can be enriching and gratifying; it can foster your development as a writer. If you decide to collaborate, you then must decide on the order of authorship and each author's specific responsibilities. Avoid confusion, misunderstanding, frustration, and disappointment spawned by a poorly decided partnership. The APA stylistic manual (American Psychological Association, 1983), for example, provides some suggestions on how to think about shared authorship, specifying the order of names appearing in by-lines, and the type of contribution agreements. The benefits of collaborative writing are well worth the attention to decision-making they require.

Selecting the type of article you write and the journal where you submit it involves decision-making. Use accurate information in choosing a type and an appropriate publication. Chapter 7 contains information to help you in the selection process.

The majority of your decisions as a writer, though, apply to the text you will create. In reality no single option exists. Rather, you face many options in organizing the text, shaping its content, and choosing the words to be used. As a writer, you determine what tone, mood, and emphasis are appropriate. You select the style, voice, and length of your text. You pick the conceptual, political, philosophical, professional, and/or practice oriented framework to use. You decide what authorities or experts to refer to in your article. Within the confines of the text you are in charge, so make such decisions wisely.

THE WRITER AS CRITIC

The last role the writer assumes is critic. As a writer you can be empowered greatly by your critiquing skills. Be a competent judge of your own writing. Evaluate it from start to finish, from idea to revised, final draft. Assess it with the detached eye of an informed reader. Employ the criteria for an effective text we presented in the previous chapter. Critically review your work both in progress and when completed.

Be realistic in your assessment. Do not be too harsh. Avoid judging your work against some imaginary, perfect article. Judge your work against comparable work. Be fair to your text and use your criticism as the raw material for improvements.

THE EFFECTIVE WRITER

Effective writers also are risk-takers as well as decision-makers. They are marked by the following:

- Curiosity
- Purposefulness
- Discipline, motivation, and commitment to task
- Organizational ability
- Openness to criticism
- Writing skill

The effective writer has a vision and recreates it for others by capturing it in language and shaping it in structure. To be an effective writer you have to be willing to practice writing as well as critique it. Comparable to the practice of medicine, the practice of writing is an imprecise mixture of art, science, skill, knowledge, intuition, and self-evaluation. The practice itself teaches the practitioner. The first step toward being an effective writer rests on committing yourself to practicing the craft.

EXERCISES

1. Make a list of all the types of writing you do. Include both personal and work related writing. Compare this list with Figure 3.1. Are there surprises? Are there other types you would enjoy?

2. Make a list of your strengths and weaknesses as a writer. Be realistic. After developing the list, convert it to a working definition of yourself as a writer and use such a definition as a guide for your initial writing efforts.

CHAPTER 4

The Writing Process

Writing is not a single act but rather a complex set of relationships, behaviors, and interactions. Writing involves cognitive, psychological, and physical dimensions. Further, it represents one of the most complicated of human activities. When you write, you use a wide range of human capabilities.

While research on composing has produced new insights about the process, we still do not fully understand the intricacies of writing. What we do know, however, can be valuable to you as you approach writing. Our purpose in this book is not to focus on the theoretical aspects of writing. Our goal is to supply you with useful knowledge about writing publishable articles.

Let's begin by taking a closer look at the composing process. As mentioned in Chapter 1, the writing process includes four distinct but related stages. These stages are sequential in nature, although at times they can overlap: Stage 1—prewriting, Stage 2—text developing, Stage 3—revising, and Stage 4—editing.

MANAGING THE PROCESS

As you approach writing a journal article or any other formal text, we recommend you assume a perspective or point of view on the writing process. This incorporates seeing the process as manageable and the writer as decision-maker. In Chapter 3 we examined the concept of a writer as decision-maker. Here we discuss the writing process as something that is manageable.

First, let's identify how manageableness applies to writing.

What do we need to manage when we write for publication? Although each writing situation has its own set of activities that must be consciously managed, we can identify a generic set for you:

- Time
- Environment
- Resources
- Task
- Manuscript
- Manuscript submission
- Reward structure

Time

When faced with the task of developing and submitting an article for publication, you will work more productively if you manage your time well. Creating and using a writing schedule which is reasonable and realistic can be a key to successful writing. Designating a specific portion of the day and a regular part of each week to writing and making a commitment to write during that period are essential.

Deadlines or benchmarks to measure accomplishment also should be established throughout the timeline you develop for yourself. Discipline yourself to meet your schedule of deadlines. Time management can and will work to your advantage if you use knowledge and realism to guide you along the way. If you are an inexperienced author and have difficulty estimating time or establishing appropriate deadlines, ask an experienced colleague to help you. Of course, a writing schedule should include flexibility to accommodate the things that can and do interfere.

Environment

Creating a writing environment that facilitates rather than inhibits your writing is essential. Part of being a productive author involves selecting and manipulating your work space and all of its dimensions. For example, one of us can look out on a farm field and a distant wooded area during the writing process so the changing seasons can serve as an antidote to too much routine. The other of us writes at the same time each day and always has easy listening music in the background.

By managing the work area, its air quality, light, sound, and decor, you can help yourself produce more text of better quality. Therefore, we urge you to manage your work environment to full personal advantage within the limitations you face.

Resources

Preparing a manuscript for publication requires resources. These resources vary from situation to situation. Some of the more typical resources writers for educational journals might rely on include the following: funding support, library materials, institutional or organizational records, government agency reports, computers or other technical assistance, and clerical support.

Knowing the capabilities and limitations of your resources can make you a better manager of them. Before you begin the writing process, ask yourself these questions: (a) What resources will I need to write this article? (b) What would it take to obtain the necessary resources? (c) Where can I find the required resources? (d) If needed resources are not available, what are the accommodations or compromises I must make? Manage your resources wisely by making them work for you rather than against you.

Task

Managing the task of writing an article for publication means asking the question, "What needs to be done?" Once you have analyzed the total task by identifying what is involved, organize the task by segmenting it into manageable parts. Tackle the task by addressing it in smaller units. Do not allow yourself to be overwhelmed by thoughts of the whole. Manage the entire process by managing each of its parts.

Manuscript

Organizing the text is essential to managing the manuscript. The use of a word processor or an outline can prove to be particularly advantageous to controlling a text as it develops. Keep in mind no one way is the correct or only way of managing a manuscript. What is required varies from writer to writer. You need to manage yours in a way that works for you.

Manuscript Submission

Submitting an article for publication is best guided by knowledge of the process. Collect all submission facts and steps required by the particular journal to which you are sending your article. Journals differ considerably in their requirements. You need to know specifically what your journal expects.

Once you have informed yourself, make a submission checklist and use it to manage the process. In Chapters 7 and 8 we detail various aspects related to the submission process.

Reward Structure

Successful management of the article development and submission process includes building in a systematic reward structure. Throughout the process recognize your accomplishments with small rewards. These simple acknowledgments serve as motivation to keep you going. Rewards can vary and need not be elaborate. They can range from taking a break to buying yourself an ice cream cone or watching television. When you write, treat yourself well and you will usually manage the task better.

WRITING PROCESS STAGES

Stage 1—Prewriting

Before rushing out to get ice cream, stop and think about what it takes to get ready to write. When does the writing process begin? What seems like a simple, direct question amounts to a difficult query. Many uninitiated writers might respond by saying, "when the first word is written." Although this answer contains some degree of accuracy, for the most part it is based on a misunderstanding of the process. Writing often begins in the mind rather than with the physical activity of crafting text. Prewriting is the first stage in the process.

Thinking and planning lie at the heart of prewriting. All writing starts with an idea and a need to put that idea in writing. Obviously without an idea writing cannot occur. Without thinking about the idea, you cannot develop it fully in a written text. Preparing yourself intellectually takes time and effort. Intellectual gestation, fostering an idea's development, and becoming comfortable with concepts of the text before actually composing promote successful text development in Stage 2.

What this means is that thought should precede formal composing. The better the thinking quality, the better the article quality. However, some writers begin with text developing (Stage 2) and move in and out of prewriting (Stage 1) simultaneously.

How can you increase the caliber of any thought involved in prewriting? Thinking skills like any others can be developed and refined. In thinking about writing, in preparing a composing idea, you can help yourself. In order to aid the thought process, focus is critical. Concentrate your attention on the following aspects:

- Subject
- Audience
- Purpose
- Use

- Technical considerations
- Planning

Subject

In order to write about any subject, you need to be interested in it to be comfortable with it. Think about the subject of your writing in various ways to fully explore the possibilities for your article. You need to consider your perspective, determine what aspects to cover, and explore how many details you will include or expand on in the text. You should identify what kind and how much preparation you will require before you can write.

Intellectual preparation varies and can include reading, researching, observing, and interviewing. Psychological preparation can mean ridding yourself of distractions or other commitments. It can involve developing a positive attitude, an enthusiasm, even a passion toward the topic and the task. Here are ways to help you organize:

1. Brainstorming or listing ideas on the topic produces valuable results. Other prewriting techniques geared to subject development are equally helpful. They include but are not limited to grouping ideas in relationship to each other.

2. Clustering involves placing the primary idea in the center of a page and establishing related terms around it. This is similar to creating a cognitive map. By circling the terms and drawing lines among and between circled items, the possible interrelationships are identified.

3. Branching is similar to clustering in providing a skeleton of relationships but relies on placing the main idea at the top of a page and placing supporting ideas below it. Leave plenty of white space between ideas. Each major idea has related minor ideas that you put to the right of corresponding major ideas. Use lines to branch out and connect minor ideas.

4. Outlining is a more developed technique, and it has many forms with varying levels of detail. It typically employs the numbering and lettering of ideas and sub-ideas. Any relationships inherent in ideas

usually are spelled out in an outline. In Chapter 9 we describe how computers can assist with outlining.

However you approach your subject, deal with it before you begin to develop a text. Invest thought and you will write with greater ease and more control.

Audience

Consider your audience before you address them in a text. Audience analysis plays an essential role in prewriting and informs decisions you will make about language, structure, and genre. Knowledge of your audience also improves your ability to write for them. A journal's stylistic guidelines often provides information on the audience.

Analyzing your audience means asking several questions:

1. Who is the audience?

2. What does my audience know?

3. What does my audience need to know?

4. What assumptions can I make about the audience?

Having a clear, well-defined sense of your primary audience will guide you in developing an article that addresses it effectively. This means engaging your readers' attention and interest. Knowing who they are facilitates your getting their ear.

Conversely, if you do not analyze your audience at the prewriting stage, your efforts to communicate with them might fail. For example, if your article describes a successful instructional practice and you submit it to a journal whose primary readership is educational researchers, it probably will get rejected as it does not address the audience. If your article is written in highly technical language and submitted to a journal read primarily by practitioners, it probably will not be accepted. The language is not the audience's language and therefore is inappropriate.

Purpose

Along with audience and subject the prewriting stage includes thinking about and planning for your intended purpose. Your purpose plays an important role in the subsequent crafting of your article. As a writer, you need to begin composing with a clear, articulated sense of where you are going. In fact, we suggest you actually state your purpose in writing. Let this statement guide your composing efforts. Allow it to keep you focused. As with knowledge of an audience, your awareness of purpose will influence a number of subsequent composing decisions.

In specifying your purpose ask yourself why you are writing. Once you have an answer to this fundamental guiding question, follow up with additional probing:

1. Am I writing to inform?

2. Am I writing to instruct?

3. Am I writing to entertain?

4. Am I writing to explain?

5. Am I writing to argue a position?

6. Am I writing to persuade?

7. Am I writing for more than one of these?

A clear sense of purpose contributes to your sense of control as a writer.

Use

Use and purpose are closely related. How an article might be used is influenced significantly but not solely by its purpose. Of course, one or more uses may emerge which are outside of your initial intention, but it is to your advantage as a writer to identify one or more potential uses of your article.

You can put knowledge of your article's potential uses and misuses to work for you when you compose. This awareness, similar to a knowledge of audience and purpose, can help you shape your text. For example, if you intend your article to be used in undergraduate clinical training for certain special education subjects, consider including concrete examples aimed at students and their faculty.

Technical Considerations

Writing entails numerous technical considerations. Before you start drafting a manuscript, determine what type of article you will write. You need to consider the journals for which your article would be best suited. Developing your text with a particular journal in mind informs decisions you will make about the text. These decisions include choices about language, form, tone, references, topics, and length. We detail various types of journal articles in Chapter 7.

Planning

Planning compliments idea generation in the prewriting stage. Along with thinking about your subject, audience, purpose, use(s), and various technical considerations, prior to creating drafts you must plan for the task. Through planning you manage your control over the task and the text.

One way of fitting time to task employs a timeline of some sort. This can be in the form of a schedule of deadlines, Gantt chart, or calendar of the various activities likely in writing your article. In designing a timeline you are plotting time against task. Of course, you need to build flexibility into the plan for those unexpected activities or delays.

In addition to focusing your planning efforts on time and task, you should also plan the text. This can take a variety of forms; the most familiar is an outline. Although an outline is a valuable tool, it is not the only one. Writing about the intended text can help to shape the text and bring insight and clarity into the process. Progoff (1975) describes the value of keeping an intensive personal journal as a mechanism for shaping text.

The form this prewriting takes can vary. It may be a journal or a log, running lists of topics, or a set of questions to be addressed by the article. Thus, when planning, be sure to include time for your prewriting activities.

Stage 2—Text Developing

The transition from prewriting to text developing can be exciting. It calls not only on your writing skills but also your creativity. Regardless of the subject, audience, purpose, and uses, as you develop a draft of your article you are engaging in highly creative intellectual activity. All things being equal, no two writers produce the same text. The distinctness of personality, talent, experience, knowledge, skill, and vision results in a unique text. You most definitely have something to write about that is uniquely yours.

Put your prewriting documents to work for you when you begin to compose. Articles can be divided into three distinct parts: the introduction, body, and conclusion. These sections apply to any type of article and as such serve as generic labels. Particular subdivisions of an article are dictated by the type of article and the specific journal to which you will submit it. Specific stylistic guidelines or expectations also are set by the journal.

In reviewing journals you will note variations in article formats and in required stylistic rules. These areas are not discretionary and left to your judgment. They are determined for writers by the journal's editors. Always use whatever is appropriate for or required by a journal to which you are submitting an article. Such information often can be found on either the front or back inside cover.

As you approach composing your first words, keep in mind you do not have to write the initial sentence of an article first. You do not even need to draft the introductory section of the text first. Begin with that part of the article with which you feel most comfortable. In essence, follow a pattern of text development which works for you.

In addition to approaching your article by sections, the

standard unit of writing is the paragraph. Although texts are written a sentence at a time, paragraphs are the fundamental organizing units. Each paragraph develops a single main idea. Every sentence in a paragraph regardless of length must relate to the main idea. Focus and consistency must be maintained within each paragraph as well as throughout each section of the article.

Transitions between paragraphs and sections contribute both to readability and coherence. If you have difficulty in moving from idea to idea, you might need to work on transitions. Effective use of language and structure can provide the linkages needed.

Introduction

An article's introductory section serves the purpose of laying necessary groundwork for the text. No single approach to writing an introduction is necessarily correct. Much depends on the type of article and corresponding journal. Introductions provide background which can be personal, historical, contextual, or situational. They also present the rationale behind a text, an overview of the article, any conceptual or guiding theoretical framework, or an author's perspective on a topic. Your prewriting efforts should guide you in selecting an introduction which best fits the article.

Your introduction should engage readers with the article by obtaining and maintaining attention and elaborating on the main point. Further, it should establish your credibility as an author by engendering in readers a sense of confidence. Without being authoritarian, you must project a voice of authority that is knowledgeable and competent from the beginning.

The introduction also serves as a place to set the article's tone. Tone is influential in establishing a positive relationship with the audience. It can vary from familiar and conversational to detached and clinical. In selecting the tone for your article, let appropriateness be your guide. Typically a conversational tone is inappropriate for a research journal and a detached tone is unacceptable in a newsletter.

Remember, too, the introduction is read first whether or not you write it first. Because of its placement in an article, the introduction is the reader's path to any substance. If the reader is blocked or diverted along this route, the article may not be read. A strong, effective introduction invites the audience to participate in your ideas. Conversely a weak, ineffective introduction can alienate the reader.

Body

The body of a text presents an article's elaborated main idea. It is the heart of your text. How the body is organized might be determined partially by any sections required in the type of article you write. In addition to the journal's organizational requirements for articles, you will need to use other patterns of paragraph organization, such as cause and effect, illustrations and examples, comparison and contrast, process, definition, and classification. Such patterns commonly function as methods for organizing and developing paragraphs, and thus the text.

The body of the text presents the elaborated discussion of your subject. Use it to full advantage by making language and structure work to increase your reader's understanding of the writer. Avoid vagueness and provide precise information, although acknowledge limitations whenever necessary. As you develop the text, again keep in mind the basics of subject, audience, purpose, and use. Do not equivocate or ramble, just elaborate purposefully and effectively.

Conclusion

An article's conclusion leads readers out of the subject by bringing any appropriate topics to some degree of satisfactory closure. In part, the type of article will determine the nature of a concluding section. Conclusions can vary. Some of the more typical kinds include but are not limited to interpretations, proposed future discussions or studies, recommendations, limitations, and a summary.

Some articles include references or suggestions for additional readings on the topic. Many readers like to continue reading on a topic and appreciate suggested readings. A journal's stylistic guidelines should describe whether or not you need to include references or reading lists with your article.

Stage 3—Revising

Although by the end of Stage 2 you have drafted your article, you have not completed the writing process until entering the revising stage. Before you begin revising, however, we suggest taking a break from the text.

During this break be proactive and seek out criticism before you submit your article for editorial consideration. We recommend you ask at least two reviewers to critique your article. Have one reader review the content and one the writing. By providing your reviewers with a direction in reading, their critique can be more focused. Further, the utility of the feedback will be enhanced.

Having ascertained reviewer feedback on your manuscript, reread the article at least three times. Begin with a global reading, reading the text as a whole from start to finish to obtain a general sense of its overall cohesiveness and clarity. Then, go back and reread it making your own critical commentary. Mark the text where you want to make changes. Make notes including questions the text raises which need addressing, terms requiring definition, references seeking elaborations, and omissions of ideas or considerations. Incorporate those suggestions made by reviewers wherever appropriate. Read it a third time looking for any remaining problems, such as inadequate transitions, inconsistencies, and inaccuracies between in-text citations and bibliographic references.

Once you have completed such readings, revise the article accordingly. Quality critical commentary and readings by you and others result in quality text. In seeing your topic again, you see it differently. Here lies the meaning of revision. The amount and type of revision you make depend on what you see. When minor changes are involved, editing is necessary. If substantive alterations are required, revision is in order.

Stage 4—Editing

Distinct from revising, which entails different ways of thinking about the topic, editing produces technical changes in the writing. In editing your text, usually the final thing done, you improve the technical quality of the writing. You correct errors in word usage, grammar, spelling, punctuation, and clarity. You might alter sentence structure slightly or rephrase a sentence or two. You might add or change transitional words and sentences. In editing your article, you clean it up and polish it for publication. Submit as perfect an article as you can.

You can edit by yourself, or use the advice of a professional editor. Either type of editing is acceptable. You make the decision about who will edit your article prior to submission. Of course, after submission and acceptance the journal editor will probably edit your text again.

FROM WRITING TO PUBLISHING

When you have negotiated all four stages successfully, you are ready to enter the publishing world. This entry can be smooth and rewarding. Although we discuss specifics of publishing in journals in Chapters 7 and 8, any discussion of the writing process is not complete without some attention to writing's companion, publishing.

During the prewriting stage, you are making preparations for submitting your article. You prepare for publishing by educating yourself about the publication process. Review appropriate journals and talk to writer-practitioners who have published. Benefit from the value of their experiences. Know that rejection is an intrinsic part of the process. Anyone who publishes regularly can tell you tales about rejection. Always remember it is the text and not you that is being judged.

Also bear in mind that reviewers are human, as is their judgment. When you embark on the process of trying to publish an article, you are making yourself vulnerable. Be prepared initially for a certain amount of anxiety and discomfort. Experience can help to counter these feelings.

Once you become a published author, there are certain responsibilities and requirements you must face. Typically you will receive galleys or page proofs of your articles just before they are to go to press with a plea from the editor for fast proofing and return. Take special care to ensure there are no errors in the manuscript, reply to any editorial questions, but return it quickly as journals normally adhere to tight deadlines.

You usually will need to make decisions about purchasing reprints of your article, unless a large number of reprints or journal copies come gratis. This is because you will obtain requests from literally all over the world for copies as some people have access only to indexing or abstracting services and not to the actual journals. This requires, too, a companion decision regarding whether or not you will communicate with those who write or call with specific questions about your articles.

The more you know about the publication process, the better equipped you are to participate in it. Have confidence in the value of what you have written. Know that you are contributing to the knowledge base of your profession. Publishing articles does not involve magic, mystery, or miracles. Rather, it is about risk-taking, commitment, confidence, and rewarding work. Commit yourself to getting your article published, the rest will follow.

EXERCISES

1. Develop a list of five questions you would like to address in your article. Next, order the questions according to the sequence your article would present them. Once ordered, generate at least two sets of responses for each question. These responses can be in phrase or sentence form. Now, turn your work into outline form. Reorganize as necessary.

2. Take what you have already written, such as a memo, report, proposal, or paper. Practice your revising skills by changing language and reworking sentences. After revision, edit it sentence by sentence and then paragraph by paragraph. Ask an editor or a colleague to review your revisions and provide you with feedback. Keep a running record of your mistakes as a reminder mechanism for reducing or not repeating them.

CHAPTER 5

The Written Product

The writing process and written product form a network of relationships with each other, the writer, and any readers. This complex network is dynamic, interactive, and generative. Text serves as a route an audience uses to relate to writers and the writing process. Figure 5.1 illustrates these writing relationships.

Your text is key to ensuring a solid working relationship. Assuming you are the writer in such a diagram, work your way through the process to your text. Then, interact with the audience through your created text. Now, visualize yourself as a reader. You are the audience. Read your way through the text. Think about what the writing process might have been like. Through this process connect with the writer.

The ingredients of text—content, structure, and perspective—constitute raw material for any text, any article. Regardless of the type of article you decide to write, you must put content together with structure and a perspective. In combining these three essentials, you initiate a textual chemistry which is uniquely your own. Your article's quality and effectiveness are measured partially on the basis of this mixture, as well as technical accuracy and appropriateness. In this chapter, we consider written text to be the product of a writer's decision making.

CONTENT

Central to any journal article is its subject. Your topic shapes your content. Indeed, content equals your topic and its

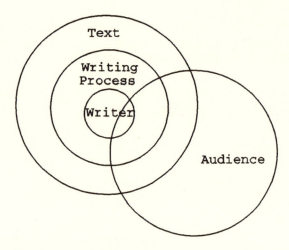

Figure 5.1 Writing relationships.

elaboration. In developing a topic you form content. As a writer considering content, ask yourself probing questions.

- Is the content valuable? Is it worthy of my writing about it?
- Is the content of interest to the audience? Is the content of interest to me?
- Is the content appropriate for the type of article?
- Is the content timely?
- Like a good film, will something of the content stay with audience members after they have read the article? Does the content contain an enduring element?

Of course, you want a predominantly positive set of responses to these questions. Let's take a closer look at each of them.

The value and worthiness of your content can serve as motivators to you as a writer. In order to invest in content you need to perceive it as worthwhile. For you to make an enthusiastic and serious commitment to developing content into an article, you must view the subject as valuable. The content need not be lofty, idealistic, or earthshaking. It does not have to break new ground professionally or make converts politically.

It should be worth the effort involved by you in writing it and by the audience in reading it. This worth does not have to be engendered universally, but rather only in you the writer and in your intended audience.

Content can be of value for many reasons. It can be useful to the reader. It can provide information, instruction, or insight. It can extend the boundaries of knowledge, skill, and understanding. Further, content's value can contribute to the development of a profession and add to the advancement or refinement of professional practice.

The worth of content also resides in its potential to stimulate thought and alter attitudes, beliefs, and values. In effecting change through developing content, as the writer you are in a powerful and responsible position. Content can and does make a difference because of its inherent value as well as the value you invest it with. The value need not be lofty nor should it be inflated, but the worth must be real.

A danger exists for beginning writers in assessing the value of their content. Many discount the worth of their subjects by thinking no one else would value them. Be fair to your intended audience. If you recognize the value of your content, know that an audience exists that would also see its worth. In elaborating any content in the article, make sure you communicate this value through the language and structure used.

Interest is comparable to value and worthiness. Interest in the content encourages you to write and your reader to read. Interest can help you surmount all kinds of obstacles to writing. Likewise, it can facilitate the audience's reading, even under less than ideal conditions. Interest in the content is a powerful motivator. Be sure you are interested in your subject.

Anything you can do to cultivate your own interest, such as talking and reading about it, will serve you well as you write. As to the interest of your audience, you can engender and cultivate interest in a subject by the way you write about it. An article's wording and form work as your vehicles for communicating with the audience. Use them to spark interest.

Matching your content to the appropriate type of article and journal is essential for a successful publication experience.

For example, assume your goal is to present an opinion on some public policy that impacts on the continuing education of social workers. After considering a range of articles, you decide an editorial piece would be most suitable. After this textual decision is made, you must review journals to find one or more that print editorial texts. Then, select a journal that seems most appropriate as your first choice.

Timeliness of the content matters because it reflects current interest in the topic. As a writer, you can promote timely appeal by how you shape the content. If your content's timeliness is not immediately apparent, you can make it so. Relate the content to a subject that currently is considered timely. In so doing, you are managing your text.

Another technique for creating this sense is to point to analogous content. Provide connections for the readers. Through linkages with related or analogous material, you can infuse your content with required timeliness. Additionally, you can invest content with timeliness by providing a new perspective on old content. We discuss perspective later in this chapter.

Finally, durability of content contributes to the role content plays in any text. Content with a potential for enduring in the readers' minds works well in engaging the audience. In elaborating your content throughout the article, be aware of ways it might replay itself beyond the reading.

STRUCTURE

Structure forms the framework, scaffolding, and skeleton of a journal article. It represents the geography and geometry of text. It refers to ideas in placement relationships with other ideas. Further, it means language in relationship with ideas or the configuration of language and ideas. As such, it is about relationships within and around the text.

Structure is composed of several dimensions, with levels that serve the systematic and organized framing of a text. In addition, structure operates on more than one level (see Figure 5.2).

The smallest level of structuring in an article is the phrase.

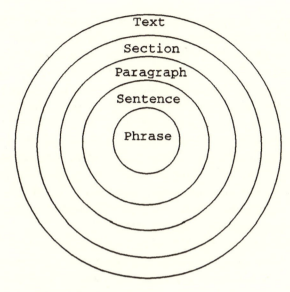

Figure 5.2 Levels of text structure.

A phrase is a group of words that functions as a unit. When you create a phrase, you form a relationship among and between the words you choose. In addition to the word relationship you make, you forge a form or a framework for organizing language and expressing content. This framework contributes to the text's meaning just as does any language used.

The next level of structure is the sentence. Sentences express complete thoughts and are made up of words and phrases. They vary in length and patterns. Thus, sentences take many shapes and contribute to the development of meaning in paragraphs and the entire article.

The paragraph is the third level of structure. Whereas at the sentence level a complete idea is presented, in a paragraph one idea is developed. Groups of related sentences make up paragraphs. Sentences within a paragraph must focus on the main idea guiding the paragraph. As a structural unit, the paragraph helps to shape the meaning underlying a subtopic or one dimension of a subtopic within an article's main topic.

Paragraphs within an article are grouped in sections, the

fourth level. The interrelatedness of linked paragraphs provide
a focus of that section. For example, if the section is about
research recommendations, it should not include paragraphs
discussing background or methods information.

In the fifth level, the article's structure emerges from a
joining of sections to make up the overall text. Integrity should
be sought in fitting together these structural pieces of your text.
A sense of unity is produced when a genuine structural integrity
exists. Often this joining is specified by either the type of article
you are writing or the journal to which you plan to submit it.

In addition to functioning on the five levels described,
structure serves other roles. Structure provides a vehicle for organizing your article. Through structure you craft your work's
logic and order the words and concepts into coherent patterns.
The structures you use contribute to a text's meaning or appropriateness in subtle ways. If not considered carefully they
can confound meaning and detract from the article's effectiveness. Keep in mind structure is one of the essential tools writers
use to manage text.

PERSPECTIVE

Inherent in any text is a perspective (more than one perspective can exist in some articles), a point of view, a writer's
angle on the topic. Your perspective is uniquely yours. Through
the altering of perspective, you can rejuvenate content and generate new insights.

Perspective speaks to the audience as does content. Your
perspective can possibly excite, provoke, or amuse the reader.
As with content, perspective can motivate the audience to read.
Perspective can also foster a meaningful relationship between
readers and the text.

In shaping your article's perspective, pay particular attention to the words and phrases you use. Be mindful of what
you choose to emphasize and project through your words. All
the points of view in an article do not necessarily need to be

your personal perspective. You will present the views, thoughts, and conclusions of others as you cite or summarize supporting literature. It is important, though, to manage all perspectives presented with consistency so readers are not confused.

Perspectives play a role in appropriate journal selection just as content does. Therefore, perspectives need to be considered when choosing your publication outlet. Certain journals may not be open to particular perspectives. For example, some journals may not publish articles taking a historical point of view. Other journals may be closed to a feminist perspective. Whatever perspective your article projects, be sure it reflects logic and connectedness in its development.

TECHNICAL ASPECTS

Content, structure, and perspective represent the broad, categorical dimensions of a text. Now we turn our discussion toward some more specifically defined elements of writing and look at the technical aspects of text. We include those areas of text which are rule bound; that is, they are either correct or incorrect. We look at matters of usage and style which play roles in textual effectiveness. In other words we examine textual mechanics and usage. Out of this exploration, we identify essential characteristics of an effective text.

In technical considerations, consult appropriate references. Technical questions about text have concrete answers. You need two basic technical reference books to write for a journal: a dictionary and the appropriate stylistic guidelines. In Chapter 8 we describe how to compile your own stylistic manual if an official one is not available. In addition to these essential resources, you may need or want a writer's manual of style, such as *The Chicago Manual of Style* (University of Chicago Press, 1982) or the *Publication Manual of the American Psychological Association* (1983).

First, let's turn our attention to those technical aspects of text that are open to judgments of correctness, those areas of your article that can be judged right or wrong. Four aspects are included among these:

1. Grammar

2. Punctuation

3. Spelling and capitalization

4. Diction

Grammar represents the relationships and function of words in a sentence. Grammatical constructions are governed by rules which can be found in a writer's handbook. This type of reference discusses the rules of grammar and provides examples of how the rules work. Since these rules are far too extensive to consider here, we simply recommend you obtain and use a good guide such as Strunk and White (1979).

Although we are not going to examine grammar in detail, we want to indicate some grammatical challenges you can encounter as a writer. Problems with grammar appear in the text development stage and can be addressed at either the revising or editing stages. Correct, functional grammar depends on your using words with the concepts of relationship and function in mind. Verbs, nouns, pronouns, adjectives, and adverbs make up the primary categories of words as they are used in sentences. Although other words, such as prepositions and articles, play roles in grammatical sentences, they do not play primary roles and often are overused.

Many grammatical errors involve the use of verbs. Foremost among these verbal problems is subject-verb agreement. Within a sentence the subject and verb must agree in number (singular or plural) and in person (first, second, or third). This particular rule has many specific elaborations as well as exceptions which we will not address. If in doubt, consult a grammar reference.

Other grammatical challenges related to verbs include but are not limited to correct use of such verbs as *to be*, verb tense, verb mood, and verb voice. Again, consult a reference when you have questions.

The appropriate use of pronouns also can test your grammatical skills. Misused pronouns introduce confusion into a text. Your point can be misunderstood or misinterpreted if you inaccurately use pronouns. Adjectives and adverbs also can raise some grammatical questions for you. Seek the answers in order to ensure your article's grammatical correctness.

In addition to grammar, the use of punctuation is governed by rules. Punctuation's grammatical function is to separate units in the text and influence meaning. As such, punctuation is purposeful, not decorative. Be directed when you punctuate a sentence. Know what purpose the punctuation serves. Know what it separates and why. Do not just insert punctuation marks to decorate the test.

Frequently used punctuation marks include the period, question mark, comma, colon, semicolon, apostrophe, quotation mark, and parenthesis. How and when these marks are employed depend on the specific textual situation. If you cannot resolve a question of punctuation, consult an appropriate reference.

Questions of spelling and capitalization are easily resolved. They are not open to creativity, although some words have variant spellings. Spelling is either correct or incorrect. Misspelling in a text is always correctable as are problems with capitalization. If you know your spelling is weak, obtain the aid of a dictionary, editor, or software spell check package.

Diction is less precise than grammar, punctuation, and spelling. Diction is word choice. It involves making decisions about the correct use or application of words you use in your article. When doubtful of a word's meaning or usage, consult the dictionary or possibly a thesaurus. Overreliance on a thesaurus, however, can result in stilted text. If your text uses terms in a peculiar way, be sure they are defined in the article.

Usage refers to the way in which words and phrases are employed in a specific form or with a particular meaning. Although related to diction in that it deals with words, usage is distinct in its meaning. Usage does not fall into a black and white technical area, rather it is gray. In matters of usage, your judgment must apply as a wide range of acceptable practices exists for the writer. Errors in usage are possible but a wide range of correct options exists.

PERSONAL STYLE

Even less precise and therefore more difficult to assess is the style of a text. Style refers to a text's overall manner and tone of expression. Unlike judging other technical aspects of your article, in order to judge your style's effectiveness, the whole article must be considered, not a particular segment. Style emerges throughout the entire text and is comprised of many elements.

In considering style there are several elements which contribute to writing effectiveness. Keep in mind that as the writer you control your article's style by managing all of its elements. In this chapter we examine ten standard ones used in a variety of contexts:

1. Organization

2. Logic

3. Coherence

4. Cohesion

5. Tone

6. Readability

7. Lexicon

8. Syntax

9. Clarity

10. Focus

Organization and logic share a reciprocal relationship and influence each other. As elements of style they are critically important because their roles are to facilitate meaning in a text. Simply put, organization refers to the orderliness of your article. Logic speaks to the reasoning inherent in the text. Together organization and logic affect an article's consistency or its coherence and cohesion. We are now describing your article's logical connections. Therefore, coherence and cohesion are necessary characteristics of effective style.

Tone also is an element of style. The stance you assume as a writer mirrors itself in the article's tone. Through the words you use and any emphasis placed on them, you project the tone. Although tone can vary within your article, in shifting it you should be guided by logic. The tone of the text should be consistent with its content and purpose and appropriate for its intended audience.

Readability constitutes an element of style often overlooked. The reading level of your article or its level of technical difficulty should be matched to the audience. Use your prewriting audience analysis to select your article's reading level. This level is determined by the text's vocabulary, or lexicon, and its syntax, the sentence structure. The more complex the syntax, the more challenging text is in terms of its readability.

You can check the readability of your article by applying a readability scale. As we note in Chapter 9, several scales for assessing readability are relatively easy to use and are available in software packages. We also detail in Chapter 7 how you can quickly calculate a readability score without a computer's help. Another, less formal method, is to have people representative of your intended audience read your article and provide you with feedback.

Your article's lexicon is important, too. Jargon, unnecessary technical words, and affected, pumped-up language are never appropriate and unduly raise readability scores. Highly technical vocabulary is appropriate given a technical audience, while it is inappropriate when the readers are outside of the technical community of discourse. The difference between technical vocabulary and jargon is in need.

Sentence structure is an aspect of syntax and should be logical and varied throughout the article. Such structure influences meaning and facilitates the audience's reading of any text. Badly ordered words within a sentence can be confusing and contribute to a lack of clarity.

Clarity in your article comes from the diction, syntax, organization, and logic. Although the elements of style can be discussed as discrete elements, in fact, they are interactive and influence each other. They do not stand alone. Clarity reflects the precision of text in its use of words and structures. Clarity also can be viewed as a function of focus.

The final element, focus, addresses the article's consistently controlled central idea. This refers to the main topic all other subtopics revolve around or to which they relate in some way. A well-managed focus is evident in its consistency and clarity. Focus keeps readers in touch with the heart of the text and writer.

Remember as you develop your style that your role is to engage the audience. The strength of your ideas is carried by your text. The text as your voice through an article is a vehicle for speaking to the reader. As such, it is a potentially powerful instrument; you must manage it well and develop it carefully.

Clearly, the effectiveness of text is critically important. In order to assess the extent your article is working, we suggest you apply several text effectiveness criteria (see Figure 5.3). They come from our discussion of an article's content, structure, perspective, and technical aspects. These criteria vary in applicability to each of these dimensions of text. Therefore, they should be used in a global reading of your article, that is, a reading of the article as a whole rather than in segments.

As the writer you should be the first critical reviewer of your article. By using the text effectiveness criteria you can systematically assess your written work. You can incorporate these criteria into your decision making as a writer with the end result being a more effective article. By applying a critical eye to your writing you can become a better writer. A carefully managed writing process produces an effective article.

EXERCISES

1. After completing a first draft of your article, go through the text. For each paragraph, label the main idea you develop. If a paragraph does not have a main idea, revise it so that

CONTENT VALUE
CONTENT INTEREST
CONTENT APPROPRIATENESS
CONTENT TIMELINESS
CONTENT DURABILITY
STRUCTURE INTEGRITY
STRUCTURE APPROPRIATENESS
PERSPECTIVE CONSISTENCY
PERSPECTIVE APPROPRIATENESS
TECHNICAL CORRECTNESS
TEXT ORGANIZATION
TEXT LOGIC
TEXT COHERENCE
TEXT COHESION
TEXT TONE
TEXT READABILITY
TEXT LEXICON
TEXT SYNTAX
TEXT CLARITY
TEXT FOCUS

Figure 5.3 Text effectiveness criteria.

it does. If it has more than one main idea, break it into two
paragraphs.

2. Make a list of the technical errors you are most likely to
   make. Keep a list of corrections consistently suggested or
   made by people who review your drafts. From these lists
   develop a checklist of what to look for as potential errors
   or problems. Apply the checklist each time you draft an article and look for specific problems in need of correction.

CHAPTER 6

Dealing With Writing Blocks

You don't know what it is to stay a whole day with your head in your hands trying to squeeze your unfortunate brain so as to find a word.

Flaubert

Squeezing the words from your unfortunate brain can be the most challenging dimension of writing. Beginning authors often find the work of writing centered in extracting the necessary words, phrases, sentences, paragraphs, and pages from their imaginations and intellects. Anyone who writes knows all too well the quantum leaps required to go from idea to text. Getting stuck between transforming a concept into words on a page or a computer screen is a familiar part of the writing process.

Writing blocks, whatever form they take (and they take a wide variety), are inherent in the writing process. Some of the annoying and frustrating obstacles reside in the writer's personality and some blocks are related to the process. In this chapter we examine both the writer's and the writing process blocks and some ways to work through them successfully. Along with consideration of obstacles which get in the way of writing, we examine writing productivity and successful strategies for increasing it by countering writing blocks.

SCENARIOS OF BLOCKED WRITERS

Imagine yourself faced with a writing task, for example, a letter, report, paper, or proposal. You think you are all set to write. You have everything you need from idea to word processor to wastebasket. What more could be necessary? You're ready. Armed with ideas and all the right support equipment, you sit down prepared to write. Sound familiar so far?

All of a sudden you feel an urgent need to clean out your files, wash the floor, clear off the top of your desk, telephone an old friend, adjust the room temperature, or make coffee. After completing this first round of what you may even recognize as delay tactics, you again prepare to settle down to the task. You put pen to paper or hands to keyboard. As if summoned from heaven you must count your paper clips and be sure all of your number two pencils are sharpened to exactly the same degree of sharpness (even though you seldom use a pencil). After you have finished with these obligations, you make your mandatory trip to the kitchen and then resume your position at the keyboard ready to work.

Having completed all of your warmup exercises, you believe you are ready to write. Now you are feeling guilty because since you first attempted to get started an hour has passed. You reprimand yourself for being a procrastinator. The self-judgment is harsh and preoccupying. Often it impedes your writing.

Finally, you begin the actual struggle of extracting a text from your brain. At this point the blankness of either the page or the screen blocks you. Thoughts of self-doubt possess you, and you keep hearing an echoing refrain, "You can't write."

Does any of this scenario hit home? It is representative of accounts reported by students, educators, and many others in such diverse fields as human services, health and medicine, education, and human resources development. Blocked writers regularly report in self-deprecating terms anecdotes describing the obstacles they face when writing. Frequently in talking about the impediments they encounter along the way to text production, they point to their specific behavior as a self-created block rather than identifying these blocks as being natural to the writing process.

WRITING BLOCKS

Let's look at what can block your writing and get in the way of productive writing. We define writing blocks as any psychological, physical, environmental, or cognitive impediments which keep a writer from producing written text.

Obstacles tend to fall into categorical types. Some blocks are internal, that is, they reside within the writer. Other blocks are outside the writer and are external in nature. Occasionally, blocks can be either internal or external, consisting of perceived or actual knowledge limitations. Regardless of any obstacle's impact on productive writing, all types of writing blocks produce frustration, anxiety, and possibly enervation.

Internal Blocks

What you believe about yourself in relation to writing can affect your writing productivity either positively or negatively. When the effect is negative, you experience a block or set of obstacles which get in the way of writing. You are unable to produce text, because you are paralyzed by the belief you cannot write, do not write well enough, do not know enough, or have nothing about which you can write.

These kinds of self-doubts can prevent you from writing. They also can pollute the writing process with frustration and stress. They can keep you from getting started or interrupt you along the way. Like a nightmarish ghost, self-doubt as a writer can psychologically haunt you, intellectually immobilize you, and regularly distract you.

In order to counter self-doubt words, you need to define yourself as a writer. "Easier said than done," you say. How do you build a working definition of yourself as a writer or prospective writer? First, start with the positive. Begin by identifying the strengths you bring to the task. Focus on the skills and knowledge you possess. Concentrate on your experience as a writer in a variety of contexts with a full range of purposes.

For example, you have written in school, at work, and at home for purposes ranging from academic, to professional, to personal. You have written in a variety of genre, including essays, letters, memos, reports, and proposals. On a less formal level, you probably write functional texts such as lists, directions, and notes. You are a writer.

Another type of internal block exists when the writer is psychologically preoccupied with something other than writing. Persistent preoccupation needs to be dealt with either by elimination cr by displacement with a psychological focus on writing and the task at hand. For example, if you have a family situation haunting you, resolve it or find out more so that you can deal with it, or block it out and free yourself to write. Replace preoccupation with the task at hand by accepting at least temporarily that you are not in a position to alter the situation.

Related to the problem of psychological preoccupations are the internal blocks writers experience because of anxieties and pressures. Unbridled stress about writing can take many shapes. For some the mere suggestion of "putting it in writing" can produce terror. Fear of failure, criticism, and intellectual or professional vulnerability commonly plagues blocked writers. Another frequently identified fear inhibited writers express is that of having nothing to write about or worth writing about.

The writer's physical condition can also obstruct the writing process. Pain, discomfort, and fatigue work against writing productivity. As with psychological distractions, physical inhibitors need remediation. They need to be treated and either resolved or mollified. An aspirin may get rid of a headache or a few hours of sleep may revitalize the body. Left untreated, physical detriments to writing can increase in strength and impact. They can expand their depth and range of obstruction when not countered.

Often physical exercise can alleviate or alter negative physical conditions. A number of short exercises ranging from walking to aerobic breathing can serve to reverse drowsiness. Something as simple as standing up and stretching can relax a body stiffened by prolonged sitting. Tired or strained eyes can benefit from a brief respite from the task or by closing them for a brief period.

External Blocks

In addition to internal blocks writers might face, they can encounter blocks of an external nature. These external blocks are environmental and reside in the writer's physical context. Environmental blocks to writing are closely related to physical ones. The environmental context in which you write can facilitate or impede your writing. The physical space, its furnishings, and its decor, be it works of art or a too full wastebasket, can have a strong effect on a writer's productivity.

Space shared with another person can create blocking problems. Another person in the room can affect the writer's ability to concentrate on the writing task or create a distraction that inhibits the writing process. Inadequate work space can keep a writer from being able to spread out the resource notes or reference cards needed to support the production of text.

Another type of block related to space is the lack of a designated writing location. Having to regularly adapt to different spaces or different environments can be handicapping. Although flexibility is valuable to any writer, stability is essential to the writing process. Having a space associated with writing serves any writer as an asset.

Similar to space, a room's lighting, temperature, and ventilation factor into writing productivity. From a negative perspective, if the room's lighting, temperature, and ventilation are inadequate or inappropriate, blocking can occur. A windowless, stuffy room dependent on poor artificial lighting may provide a set of environmental conditions aimed at obstructing. On the other hand, for some writers windows may open opportunities for distractions and get in the way of the task.

Sound can also play a role in blocking. Sound affects each writer differently. Some writers need sound, others are impeded by it. The amount and type of sound a writer can use to advantage or disadvantage varies tremendously. Too much background talking or silence can create blocks, just as vocal music or no music can. The specifics of sounds that block are highly idiosyncratic.

Use sound to your advantage when writing. If a particular type of music stimulates your writing, be sure to listen to it. If sound distracts or disturbs you when you write, then avoid it as much as possible.

Since blocked writers often identify environmental obstacles to writing, selecting the environment that works best for you can produce positive results. Conversely, the wrong kind of environment has the potential of blocking you.

Knowledge Blocks

In addition to various internal or external blocks, knowledge issues can inhibit writing. Cognitive problems may even lead to total paralysis or periodic interruption of your writing.

Cognitive or knowledge obstacles take a variety of forms. The more common types relate to inadequate knowledge about a particular writing task or topic. This often means underdeveloped skills in higher order thinking. The greater your knowledge of the subject and task, the more empowered you are to tackle the subsequent writing. The less you know or think you know, the greater a potential for being blocked in developing a text. In essence, for writers knowledge is power. Without adequate knowledge writing may be impossible.

Writers frequently identify blocks which are cognitive in nature. A common example involves premature initiation of a task. Simply put, a writer attempting to write too soon before ideas behind the necessary text are developed adequately may soon be blocked. In order to write with ease, to find the appropriate language, structure, and organizational patterns, you need to acquire a certain level of familiarity, comfort, and command of your topic and writing genre.

Intellectual gestation is an essential ingredient of productive writing. The ideas and the form of expressing them have to be ready for written articulation. Prematurely trying to write can result in a block if the expectation is to create a polished text. If the goal is to use writing to learn rather than to communicate, however, then writing can be used as a way of reaching clarity, exploring ideas, and coming to know your subject.

Writing may also be a way of testing or clarifying your ideas. Be clear on and aware of your own purpose in writing. Before you are intellectually ready to produce a working draft, view writing as a way to learn more about your topic. Use it as a vehicle to produce ideas and newly learned knowledge. In other words, do not view writing as a way to communicate formally with an external audience, rather think of it as a way of passing on information to others.

Change your thinking about writing and the experience itself will change. In this situation, the change should be to your advantage. By putting those prewriting activities we described in Chapter 4 to work for you, cognitive blocks can be avoided or eliminated. By approaching writing with a clear and realistic sense of purpose, you can gain greater control over the written product and the writing process.

OVERCOMING WRITING BLOCKS

Whatever form writing blocks take, they are not insurmountable. The ways to deal with blocks are as numerous and varied as the obstacles themselves. Impediments to writing, assuming intelligence and skill on the part of the writer, are treatable. Appropriate interventions can resolve a writing block and thus free you of the accompanying anxiety, frustration, and self-doubt.

Finding the most effective unblocking strategy to fit the specifics of a situation might take some experimentation and even a willingness to take risks. No single correct approach to unblocking exists. Many techniques work. You need to find ones that will work for you.

Initially you should try applying different techniques for unblocking until you discover a strategy that is well suited to the problem. The same strategy probably will not work with every obstacle, just as the same technique will not work equally well for every writer. The solution should fit the writer as well as the writing. Because the writing process is so highly idiosyncratic and individualistic, absolutes are impossible. The following sections identify various strategies you can try for each source.

Physical Source Strategies

Writing blocks rooted in physical sources often, though not always, have simple solutions. For example, writing can be blocked by persistent basic human needs, such as hunger. A growling stomach may deprive you of your ability to concentrate on writing. The hungrier you get, the more distracted you become. Eat and satisfy the hunger.

A related need is for periodic and regular rest to capitalize on your most intellectually productive time of day. Knowing your best time to write and accommodating it can pay off in fewer obstacles to writing as well as in higher quality text.

Health also plays a role in being a productive writer. Writers can get stuck when plagued with health problems. Wellness contributes to a generative writing experience. Remedy those problems which are treatable and accommodate those that are not.

Psychological Source Strategies

Overcoming psychological blocks to writing is not as illusive as it may seem. Identifying any roots of a psychological obstacle, however challenging, is important. Knowing whether your paralyzing stress is embedded in a fear of the text being open to criticism or a need to produce the perfect manuscript holds a key to determining an appropriate intervention. In order to unblock, you need to know the source and nature of any psychological block.

Psychologically based blocks exist in many forms. For example, fear inhibits many writers. These fears possess a myriad of faces. Among the more common facades are fear of failure and fear of criticism. The vulnerability endemic to any writer's experience freezes some and keeps them from producing text. Accepting writing as a potentially rewarding and enriching risk-taking process can modify the negative effects of these fears by freeing the writer to write.

Indeed, you can learn to welcome criticism as a way to develop as a writer and as a vehicle for improving texts. Learn to take the psychological offensive in regard to vulnerability and criticism. Seek critical feedback at all stages of the process. Learn to be comfortable with risk. Remember the text, not the writer, is under review.

Anxiety, like fear, comes in many varieties and works in much the same way. It can cripple a writer. For instance, some writers get anxious over deadlines. The thought of having to complete a text or part of a text by a certain date can create stress and intellectual paralysis. Take charge of imposed deadlines. As we noted in Chapter 4, make your own Gantt chart or timeline of important activities.

By imposing your own timeline, you can accomplish two goals. First, you gain greater control over the writing process by diminishing the power of any externally determined deadline. Second, you often artificially add time and a safety valve to the time available. In so doing, you have taken control of the process and empowered yourself as a writer.

In addition to anxiety over deadlines, writers identify obstructions generated from being overwhelmed by the whole writing task. If developing an entire article seems too burdensome, break the text into manageable parts. Managing the text is a key to developing it. Gaining control results in anxiety reduction.

Another kind of anxiety encountered especially by novice writers comes from inexperience. When the topic or genre is new to a writer, anxiety about writing can be debilitating. Text development can suffer. It is not at all uncommon for writers to feel intimidated by an encounter with a new or an unfamiliar type of writing. An effective strategy for breaking through this type of block is acquiring experience with the topic or genre through reading. Build familiarity by critically examining some article written in the style you wish to emulate or on the topic in which you are interested. The confidence gained frequently is enough to reduce any debilitating anxiety.

Experience can work negatively and produce anxiety in another way. Past experience with writing of a less-than-positive nature often results in anxiety. In turn, this historically generated anxiety interferes with the writer developing text. Allow yourself the benefit of growth, development, and change to conquer such anxiety. Move forward by recalling positive intellectual and professional experiences that included some writing. Use these positive ones to displace any negative ones.

Since writing involves a commitment, it has the power to create strong anxiety. Freezing in the face of writing can be the direct result of commitment-related anxiety. For some individuals, writing is viewed as permanent, and as such, it requires perfection. When viewed instead as a process, writing holds the capacity to change, develop, improve, and engage the writer.

Like any relationship, writing benefits from openness. You need not be hostage to your writing. Commitment to the task of writing has the power to open you to various possibilities. A successful technique for working beyond anxiety involves keeping a journal or log as you write. Monitor your own progress. This strategy will help to keep you on task, as well as counter the anxiety by processing and managing it. Also, as we have noted before, journals, logs, or diaries may stimulate writing.

Another psychologically based block involves problems with self-concept or self-definition. If you are new at writing for professional audiences, defining yourself as a writer is particularly important. Your knowledge and experience provide you with the substance for writing. Use such substance to advantage in forming a concept of yourself as a writer with something valuable to communicate to colleagues. Give yourself power as a practitioner by revising your professional self-definition to include the role of writer.

On rare occasions you may encounter a psychological block whose strength is so powerful it necessitates professional intervention. Such writing blocks can be treated clinically with success. Most writing blocks, though, are not this severe and can be remedied given careful self-analysis and knowledge of effective unblocking strategies.

Environmental Source Strategies

Blocks originating in a writer's environment are often easily eliminated. A generic strategy covers a multitude of contextually based obstacles to writing. Simply put, if something in your environment keeps you from productive writing, then change or alter the environment.

To the extent possible, control the environment. Have a place well suited to your particular writing needs. To be most productive as a writer, define a particular environment as your writing place. The ideal environment is usually not possible so you must learn to adapt to what is available. Flexibility is essential to any writer.

Cognitive Source Strategies

Writing blocks grounded in cognition involve knowledge and skills. Insufficient knowledge or inadequate writing skills can have a substantial negative impact on text development and can obstruct your writing from the moment you start.

If such deficiencies keep you from writing, several strategies can help. Educate yourself through reading, attending courses, workshops or seminars, and networking with productive colleagues. Use the resources, human and otherwise, available to you to increase your knowledge and skills. Try collaborating with a colleague whose skills, knowledge, and talent will enhance the writing process. Seek the advice of a writing consultant or editor. Talk or write about the writing task and convert appropriate segments of the discussion into text or use it as a stimulant for text development. You may even be able to analyze your cognitive strengths and weaknesses by listing what you know, what you need to know, and what potential resources are needed to fill the gap.

Additional Strategies

As we described in Chapter 4, a number of prewriting activities may serve as unblocking techniques. These include freewriting, brainstorming, outlining, keeping a journal, making lists of words, phrases, and ideas, and developing related questions.

Writing about writing, describing the task, and exploring the topic constitute additional ways of facilitating stalled writers. If you speak with ease but write with difficulty, try a tape recorder. Using the recorder to make commentary on the process or to talk about your text can be extremely positive. By transcribing the text on tape, you will have a written draft to work with and revise.

These suggested strategies for blocked writers address a wide range of possibilities. Effectiveness is increased by matching strategy to your personality and particular writing block. What works in one situation may not work in another. Having a repertoire of unblocking techniques will contribute to your writing productivity and your development as a writer. As with any intellectual challenge, take the offensive, gain control over the tasks, and manage the process. Be sure to establish and maintain a writing momentum. Reward yourself regularly throughout the writing process. Recognize the worth of your own ideas and experience and write, write, write.

EXERCISES

1. Imagine yourself in a writing situation. You are faced with a writing task. You are blocked. Recreate the picture on paper by identifying everything you can remember. Using

this visual image, develop a list of strategies or approaches that would make writing more possible.

2. Using the above exercise, look within yourself rather than at the external picture. Identify what you are thinking, knowing, and feeling. Identify all the ritualistic or regular behaviors you exhibit as you approach a writing task. Develop a written list from your analysis. Then generate a list of strategies which could get you writing again.

CHAPTER 7

Preparing Manuscripts

Preparing a manuscript for submission involves careful attention to the target journal's stylistic requirements and author's guidelines. All journals adhere to rules of style. Frequently these requirements are adapted from scholarly and professional associations' rules of style (such as the American Psychological Association, Council of Biology Editors, or Modern Language Association). Editors and journal reviewers apply the stylistic rules to the review process in exercising their roles as monitors of quality control. Inattention to these rules of style can and often does result in an editor rejecting the manuscript. On the other hand, attending to the journal's guidelines and rules for authors can contribute to your manuscript's success in the publication arena.

This chapter aims at increasing your potential for successfully negotiating the process. We focus on how to prepare your article for submission to a periodical. We point out what to consider in selecting an appropriate journal for your article. We discuss stylistic guidelines as well as manuscript preparation. Careful manuscript preparation and journal selection are essential elements in the successful publication process.

SELECTING THE PERIODICAL

Selecting the best journal for your article is important in that several journals may be possibilities. If you are not familiar with the range of possible periodicals, study several journals to determine what they are looking for and the types of articles they accept. There are sources that can help you in this decision-making process. As one example, adult educators can turn to an index published by the Office of Research and Evaluation in Adult and Continuing Education at Northern Illinois University (1989). This publication lists more than 160 English language periodicals interested in articles related to adult education, although many other subject matter areas are included, too. It is updated periodically.

Remember that regionally based journals may be appropriate outlets for your articles, either because their editors are looking for region-specific information to disseminate or they want their readers to be exposed to ideas of national significance. Adult educators, for example, have two regional journals that seek articles from throughout North America: The Mountain Plains *Journal of Adult Education* housed at the University of Wyoming and the Pennsylvania *Journal of Lifelong Learning* housed at Indiana University of Pennsylvania. Both periodicals are refereed.

Other sources of potential help are Brunk (1989), Mullins (1977), and Marquis Academic Media (1981). Be aware that periodicals can cease operation depending on their financial feasibility or they may change focus over time. The best advice is to examine current issues of any periodical in which you are interested.

When examining a recent issue, especially a periodical with which you are not already acquainted, look for helpful information already provided by an editor. Many journals contain a statement in each issue or refer you to an issue that contains a purpose statement, describes the types of articles sought, and provides other useful information. If your article primarily reports experimental research but the magazine you are examining only wants practice-oriented pieces, then it makes little sense to spend time submitting to that journal.

There will be times, though, when it is not clear from printed comments the specific areas in which a journal is interested. Then we recommend you carry out an informal content analysis. Always look at more than one issue of the journal in this process, if possible, to obtain a realistic understanding of expectations and products. One purpose is to determine information about articles published such as their methodology, style, and content. Consider creating a matrix or table that includes information on each article in two or more issues. This informal analysis could cover such topics as those depicted in Table 7.1, or you can choose those that better fit your needs. Such an analysis provides considerable information about what a particular journal is publishing.

STYLISTIC GUIDELINES

It is very important that you adhere closely to a selected periodical's stylistic guidelines. Some journals publish their guidelines each time or provide information in each issue on how to obtain them. You may need to contact the editor of certain journals and have the guidelines sent. Include a stamped, self-addressed envelope if you are doing this by mail. Northern Illinois University's index also contains such information as editorial policies, average article length, and frequency of publication for the journals analyzed. We recommend compiling specific information on any journal in which you are interested. Figure 7.1 suggests a summary format for this task.

Some journals require that you adhere strictly to a specific set of stylistic guidelines. For example, many journals related to education require that all articles adhere to the American Psychological Association's (APA) current stylistic manual (1983). If you plan to submit articles frequently to such journals, we encourage you to acquire a copy of the APA manual. The manual contains pages of a simulated article written in the APA style (Figure 7 in the manual's Chapter 4) that you can use as a generic guide for your own article if you have never written one for this format. The association also sells a video tape that demonstrates how to use its guidelines. It should be noted that many APA requirements are open to interpretation and any journal might have special requirements or adaptations.

Table 7.1. Analysis of a Journal's Intent

Journal Name:	Adult Education Quarterly	

Content Description of Each Article	Information Gathering Methodology Used	Style Used
Vol. 42, Winter, 1991:		
1. International—Adult education in The Netherlands	Case study—recent historical information	Historical comparative discussion
2. Developing criteria for theory building in adult education	Personal experience, discussion with others, critical thinking	Personalized conceptual development
3. Nurse participation in baccalaureate nursing programs	In-depth interviews and completion of force field diagrams	Qualitative model building
4. Meaning of adult education in the United States	Historical research	Historical discussion
Vol. 42, Spring, 1992:		
1. Understanding AIDS themes to promote good practices for learners	Content analysis of several magazines and newspapers	Construct development
2. Comparing critical thinking and self-directed learning theoretical frameworks	Personalized comparison and derivation of linkages	Theoretical framework development
3. Self-education as a model for adult education	Personalized evaluation of existing and needed adult education models	Critique and theoretical development
4. Assessment of a staged self-directed learning model	Personalized evaluation of proposed adult education models	Critique

The issue also includes two essay reviews of several books on common themes.

Journal/Magazine Name _____

Contact Information:

    Editor's name _____

    Address _____

        _____

        _____

    Phone/FAX _____

    Email ID _____

Submission Guideline Information:

    Style used _____

    No. of copies _____

    Margins needed _____

Publication Information:

    Frequency _____

    Deadlines _____

Review Information:

    Review type _____

    Time allowed _____

Legal Requirements:

    Warrant needed _____

    Permissions _____

Other Needs _____

_____

_____

Figure 7.1 Periodical summary information.

If you cannot obtain information on stylistic requirements, create your own guidelines by carrying out a stylistic analysis of several articles in at least two issues of the journal. If you want a true picture of all types a journal seeks, you should analyze all the articles in several issues. If you desire to deter-

Journal Name			
Article Title and Dates	1.	2.	3.
Seriation Style:			

Type of Heading:
  1st Order
  2nd Order
  3rd Order			

Quoting Format:			

Estimations:
  Average Words
  Average Pages			

References:
  No. per article
  Style used			

Format for Tables:			
Format for Figures:			
Other Visuals Used:			
Readability Scale Information:			

Citations:
  No. per article
  Style used			

Special needs:			
Comments:			

Figure 7.2 Creating a journal's stylistic guidelines.

mine how a particular type of article is formatted, you may need to seek out several issues and focus only on that type.

The procedure involves analyzing several characteristics or features. Figure 7.2 provides some suggestions for you to consider. Examine the categories for each article selected and then compile a range, average, and overall description or conclusion where appropriate. To determine specific stylistic peculiarities, examine how seriation within or by paragraph takes place. How are headings used in terms of centering, capitalization, and underlining? Are quotes offset? What is the average number of words per article? How are authors referenced within the text? How are figures or tables designed?

Determine how references are formatted. Are states abbreviated when publishing information is presented? How are commas, semicolons, and colons used? When is capitalization used and when is it not? What type of abbreviations are used or expected?

You may desire to add other categories if the information is available, such as publication schedule, review process used, and number of copies required. The main point is to obtain as much precise information as possible regarding the journal's expectations and actual practice so you can match them in your own efforts. If you discover most articles do not contain figures or tables or they are under an estimated 4,000 words, it would not make sense to send the journal an article of 6,000 or more words that contained several figures and tables. We also recommend you calculate by hand or via computer software some of the indices available for analyzing writing, such as a readability scale. Rightwriter® 3.1 software used for analyzing grammar and style, for example, analyzes written material and computes several indices, including a readability scale score.

If you don't have access to appropriate computer software, here are steps you can follow to compute what Gunning (1968) calls a readability appraisal or fog index:

1. Select a sample of your text (at least 100 words).

2. Count the number of words (treat hyphenated words, numbers, abbreviations, and symbols as a single word).

3. Count the number of sentences.

4. Determine the average number of words per sentence.

5. Count the number of hard words (treat all words of three or more syllables, abbreviations, and symbols as hard words).

6. Determine the percentage of hard words.

7. Add together the word average and percent number.

8. Multiply that sum by .4, a readability factor determined by Gunning.

The result roughly approximates grade level. A score of 12.2 would indicate that the material is aimed at an audience with a high school education.

Apply the fog index steps or a computerized readability scale to one or more passages selected at random from articles in the journal to which you wish to submit your article. Compare such results with similar scores from your own writing to determine if you need to raise or lower your score. Scores can be lowered by using simpler words, the active voice, shorter sentences, single thought sentences, and only necessary words. If you know the average readability scale for a particular journal, craft your article to fit what the editors are seeking.

MANUSCRIPT PREPARATION

When you understand what a journal expects and requires, you can shape your article accordingly. Chapter 8 provides considerable information pertaining to planning an article and the author's role in writing it. The APA manual (American Psychological Association, 1983) contains a useful manuscript preparation checklist on the inside of both front and back covers.

Permission to include previously published figures, graphs, tables, or other illustrations needs to be obtained unless the material is in the public domain. Under current copyright law you may quote small sections from published materials without obtaining permission, but the number of quoted words allowed in an article will vary from publisher to publisher. Most stylistic guidelines contain such information. Figure 7.3 is a form you could adapt for obtaining any needed permissions.

We also recommend you pay particular attention to the word length or page limitations imposed by a journal whether

PERMISSION REQUEST   Date _____

Permission Department   Return the Request to:

_____   _____
_____   _____
_____   _____

I am preparing a manuscript for an article entitled:

_____

to be submitted for publication in [name of journal],

published by _____ [name of publisher] _____

I request your permission to use the following material from:

Title: _____

Author: _____

No. of words: _____ On pages numbered _____

Opening words: _____

Closing words: _____

Table No.(s): _____ On pages numbered _____

Figure No.(s): _____ On pages numbered _____

Journal Readership: _____

Proposed credit line: ____ [place something like Reprinted by ____

___ permission of (name of publishing company).] _____

                          Signed: _____
                          Name: _____
                          Address: _____

                                  _____
- -
We hereby grant permission for use of the above-mentioned material.

Date: _____   Signed: _____

                                   _____

If proposed credit line is inadequate, please specify requirements:

_____
_____
_____

An extra copy is included for your records. Thank you!

Figure 7.3 Sample permission request form.

it is published in their guidelines or is something you estimate from an informal analysis. In Chapters 8 and 10, we discuss space limitations and ways to reduce the number of words in an article.

Finally, take special care in ensuring the use of inclusive language throughout your article. Some periodicals require that you remove all gender bias, such as gender-specific pronouns, from your article before submission. The APA manual described earlier has a section devoted to avoiding gender, ethnic bias, and stereotyped characterizations. Appendix A in this book contains a sample of how necessary corrections can be made.

The preparation of manuscripts for submission to journals and magazines is not difficult, but it usually requires you to follow certain style and formatting guidelines that may change from one periodical to another. We urge you to become familiar with such guidelines during your prewriting activities. This will save you considerable frustration and possible rewriting time at a later point.

EXERCISES

1. Select several periodicals in which you are interested and seek the stylistic guidelines for each. Some journals will publish their guidelines in each issue or periodically and you can photocopy them. Other journals will tell you how to obtain the information or will refer you to some standard guide.

2. Utilize Figures 7.1 and 7.2, or your adaptation of these forms, and analyze at least three articles in some journal in which you would like to publish but for which you cannot find stylistic guidelines. Develop a guide that details what you need to know about style, format, and publishing requirements prior to submitting an article.

CHAPTER 8

The Manuscript Submission Process

Submitting a manuscript for publication entails more than just sending it to any magazine or journal you find interesting. Before submitting your article, you must know something about the periodical's procedures, expectations, and stylistic requirements. You also should understand the roles played by editors and, if it is refereed, something about the reviewers' roles. You should carefully plan, establish a timeline, and commit yourself to follow your plans. This chapter presents facts about and strategies applicable to the manuscript submission process.

THE RANGE OF EDUCATION-RELATED PERIODICALS

Education-related articles appear in a wide range of journals and magazines. Some periodicals concentrate on specific subjects or content, such as counseling, gerontology, or technology. As a prospective author, you need to understand well a journal's audience, purposes, and uses. Some journals are broad and aim at diverse practitioners or researchers who in some way work with educational programs. Many journals focus mainly on youth or adults, although some accept articles covering all ages.

This chapter incorporates an informal assessment of two recent issues for each of thirty professional periodicals as illustrative. They represent a broad spectrum of publications with education-related articles on various topics and interest areas aimed at different audiences.[1] More than 500 articles were examined. They included research reports, theoretical formulations, reviews, and essays. Various topics, methodological approaches, and writing styles were represented in this study. Obviously, selecting a different set would result in a different list, so carry out a similar exercise with journals of your own interest.

This assessment revealed useful findings. An average of about nine articles per issue was found, although the range was three to twenty-two. Some articles spanned fewer than two pages, while some had between thirty to thirty-five pages. The average length was fourteen pages or nearly 9,000 words. One journal accepted manuscripts of up to 16,000 words. Many journals, though, stressed the desire for short articles. Because space usually is at a premium, a useful rule of thumb is make your articles as short as possible while maintaining a quality product. Economy of language and syntax are valued by editors.

Journal Types

Generally, you will consider one of two periodical categories for your article. The first includes practitioner-oriented journals or magazines. Such periodicals emphasize a practical approach. They may provide specific discussions of educational procedures, advice on working with learners, or accounts of how research informs practice. Such publications often are not reviewed by external readers, but instead are handled by in-house editorial staff. It is not unusual for one or more articles per issue to be commissioned, invited, or written by a staff member. These periodicals frequently use photographs, and have a slicker look to them. Many are published eight to twelve times annually.

The second broad journal category includes research journals. These publications usually report the results of discrete research efforts. Research to practice advice often is absent or given little attention. They also normally employ a refereed or blind review process (described later in this chapter). Generally articles are longer than those in practitioner journals, include more specialized terminology, contain supporting visuals such as figures or tables, and are published four or fewer times annually.

Article Types

Education-related articles cover a wide range. Figure 8.1 presents various possibilities. Some periodicals publish articles in more than one category. You may know of a type that does not fit any of those described. If so, you need to check each journal you find interesting for specific expectations and potential models related to your own article.

A new development is taking place that is changing the way authors think about selecting journals and types of articles to write. This growing trend is the establishment of electronic journals. Usually these journals handle everything electronically. For example, *New Horizons in Adult Education* is a refereed electronic journal currently published by Nova University. People in several countries serve as editorial board members. The journal is transmitted to readers via Bitnet, Internet, or associated networks. Other electronic journals are being published or developed so this phenomenon presents new outlets and formats for your articles.

THE REVIEW PROCESS

The review process differs somewhat across journals, but some common procedures are used by most editors. Initially, when an article is received by a journal, it is logged. This procedure includes adding identifying numbers, checking for reasonable adherence to required stylistic guidelines, determining if necessary warrant releases or permissions have been included, and scanning the manuscript to determine its appropriateness for the journal. Some journals have a policy of returning articles if they deviate too far from stylistic or editorial expectations. As noted in Chapter 7, find out everything you can about the review process before submitting an article.

DATA COLLECTION/ANALYSIS APPROACHES

Educational Foundation Reports
    Biographical Research
    Historical Research
    International/Comparative Study
    Philosophical Analysis

Qualitative Reports
    Case Studies
    Ethnographic Reports
    Field Reports
    Grounded Theory Development
    Personal Interviews

Quantitative Reports
    Concept/Content Analysis
    Experimental Research
    Multivariate Analysis
    Survey Research

PRACTICAL APPLICATIONS

Applied Research Report or Analysis
    A "How-To" or "Show and Tell" Essay
    Application of Theory to Practice
    Concept Paper/Report
    Practitioner's Guide
    Report of Classroom Experience
    Special Case Report
    Practice Techniques/Advice

Critical Reviews/Reflections
    Annotated and Interpretive Bibliographies
    Article Critique
    Book/Media/Resources Review
    Critical Analysis of Some Research or Theory Area
    Essay/Interpretive Literature Review
    Forum Essay

Theory Building Reports
    Conceptual Understanding
    Theory Advancement/Formulation
    Theoretical Implications
    Theoretical Synthesis

MISCELLANEOUS

    Analysis of Technological Teaching Approach
    Ethical Assessment/Formulation/Interpretation
    Evaluation Report
    Interview of a Person
    Leadership Guidelines
    Life History or Autobiographical Report
    Personal Beliefs
    Policy Analysis or Development

Figure 8.1 Range of article types.

The Refereed Review

After initial screening, reviews usually focus on content, accuracy, significance, and tightness of fit with the journal. Many periodicals use what is commonly known as a refereed, blind, or peer review process. Referees are professionals in the field represented by a journal who generally are widely published, have editorial experience and special content expertise, or otherwise are judged appropriate by the editor.

The term *blind review* pivots on the notion that people can review manuscripts more objectively if they cannot identify the names of any authors. Thus, in a refereed review, the editor or a staff person first removes all references to authors' names before sending an article to reviewers. Some periodicals require that authors prepare articles for blind review by submitting copies that have already masked all identifying information.

The refereeing process is quite important to many professionals where promotions are associated with scholarly productivity. Referees are expected to ascertain whether a manuscript adheres to certain scholarly standards, is methodologically correct, and contributes new knowledge to the discipline or profession. They employ such criteria as assessing importance of the problem being addressed, ascertaining linkages to relevant literature, analyzing data collection appropriateness, determining if findings reported are consistent and accurate, and evaluating pertinence of any conclusions. Some reviewers also critique articles in terms of readability, although editorial staffs ordinarily deal with specific editorial concerns.

Peer reviewers make one of four decisions: accept, conditional acceptance based on needed revisions, reject but encourage resubmission if certain major flaws can be corrected, or reject. Most editors provide you with specific rewriting suggestions if your article is not accepted. Follow these suggestions, if possible, and resubmit quickly if you have been encouraged to do so.

The value of refereeing is that if you follow any advice given or communicate well why you disagree with a suggestion, the chance of acceptance in a second round of reviews is greatly enhanced. Even if you have not been encouraged to resubmit, the critique provided usually results in an improved article that may be accepted by another journal. If you have any questions about the editorial decision or the review comments, you should contact the editor for clarification.

A Non-Refereed Review

The second commonly used review procedure is a non-refereed process. This assessment can involve the review of a manuscript by one or more internal editorial staff members. Such reviewers are ensuring the manuscript is well written, within the journal's scope, fits regular departments, matches thematic needs, and/or will be of interest to readers. Such evaluative criteria as originality, audience appeal, practicality, readability, and contribution potential may be used.

Although thought by some scholars to be less rigorous or objective, such publication efforts have value in presenting practical discussions, providing summaries of research findings, considering new information on topics important to the field, promoting new ideas, and offering commentary by the field's leaders to the readership. A non-refereed periodical can be a good place to begin your publishing efforts. Frequently such periodicals have more readers than the more research-oriented ones.

PLANNING ARTICLE SUBMISSION

What comes first, writing the article or selecting the journal? Some experienced authors suggest writing the article and then finding a periodical appropriate for submission. Others recommend finding a journal that is soliciting articles on some theme and write for it. As part of your Stage 1 activities (the four stages to successful writing are introduced in Chapter 1), we recommend you take a deliberate route involving some searching, planning, and crafting. Figure 8.2 suggests a planning

1. Potential type of article:

2. Article purposes:

3. Targeted audience:

4. Probable primary journal:

5. Secondary journal:

6. Describe primary journal's stylistic expectations:

7. Planned data and literature reference basis:

8. Develop a tentative summary or abstract of the article, an outline of
   major headings, description of the problem, major points to be made,
   method or approach used, potential implications, and a time line.

Figure 8.2 A planning summary for your proposed article.

format. It assumes that you have done a skillful job in carrying
out any necessary research, reviewing relevant literature, and
thinking about the implications of your efforts. These planning
activities can and often do develop with prewriting.

To begin your planning, determine the type of article you
would like to write (see Figure 8.1). Your data or content sometimes dictates a fairly narrow range of possibilities. Then identify one or more primary purposes for your article. You may
wish to review a book and write an interpretive critique. You
might wish to venture into uncharted areas with your thinking
and develop an essay. You may desire to convert your disser-
tation research into a published format. Keep a potential audience in mind as you develop your article.

As part of your planning, search for an appropriate journal
for your manuscript. This step may involve some of the procedures described in Chapter 7. We also recommend selecting one
or more publications as secondary choices. Chapter 10 describes
a 3 by 3 rule of thumb for thinking about journal and article
possibilities.

As we pointed out in Chapter 7, it is important to understand everything you can about the stylistic requirements of any journals you consider. Record the rules or guidelines that differ significantly from those you frequently use. Describe the data, information, and literature you will use. You may not know everything initially, but attempting descriptions early is helpful in bringing some cohesion to the article.

After you have planned you need to accept some specific responsibilities. Occasionally, stylistic guidelines recommend or require that you query the editor about your idea before submitting to determine its feasibility. Check this as soon as you have completed your initial planning. It should be noted, though, that some editors will not have the time or resources to review queries.

In Chapter 4 we described Stage 2, the writing process, in detail. As an author you need to be familiar with what it takes for text development. Once you have gone through the writing process, including Stages 3 and 4 where you finalize a high quality manuscript, you are ready for the submission process.

Now you should have a final copy ready for submittal, one that adheres to all the journal's technical requirements. After you have prepared the required number of professional-looking copies, develop a cover letter. This letter should notify the editor that you have followed the stylistic guidelines, describe why you have directed your article to the journal, and provide any qualifications. Appendix B contains a sample cover letter.

Many stylistic guidelines require that you submit a warrant statement guaranteeing a single submission of the article. Ethical issues, such as those covered by warrant statements, are discussed in Chapter 10.

THE EDITOR'S ROLE

An editor must play many roles to ensure that a quality publication is published on schedule, remains financially feasible, and is read by subscribers. Perhaps the most important of these functions is what Hubbard (1989) describes as finding a "window in the sky" through which articles pass. In essence, this term refers to knowing well the journal's readers, the associated professional discipline, and the kinds of articles that must fit that window to maintain viability.

Some editors look for articles with broad appeal. Some look for manuscripts appealing to special interest groups, such as literacy or gerontology professionals. Many journals conduct regular readership surveys to keep in touch with their audience so you should always look for the most recent statement of purpose.

A usual editorial practice is to have three to four issues laid out in advance on a storyboard. This practice makes it possible for the editors to place accepted articles within an expanded timeframe and also meet requirements for variety. They can keep track of special interest articles so that over a year many different areas or topics can be addressed.

Editors work with authors in a variety of ways. Most commonly, editors manage communication about the processing, progress, and disposition of submitted articles. Editors seek authors for specialized topics. They sometimes contact people who have made conference presentations of potential interest to readers and encourage them to develop a corresponding article. Most editors develop an instinct for what will make good articles for their journals. Often this means encouraging beginning authors to put their thoughts into publishable forms.

Editors write many letters to authors regarding rejections or encouragements for resubmissions. Most editors take special care with such letters to ensure reviewers' comments are summarized, ideas for improvement are clearly transmitted, and other journals are recommended as possible outlets if appropriate. It is this fine tuning of accepted or prospective works that keeps the quality of a journal high.

An editor usually shoulders some administrative responsibility for the journal. This role includes conducting an annual review of the periodical, representing it at professional meetings, conducting writing workshops, and maintaining the periodical's strength and position. It may involve obtaining or replacing re-

viewers and providing them with feedback on their perfor-
mance.

Finally, you should know that many editors of professional
journals related to education serve gratis or with little compen-
sation for their actual time spent. Most have many other professional responsibilities. As a result the speed with which your
article gets handled and the submission procedure's formal requirements may be affected accordingly.

REVIEWERS' ROLES

Many journals have an established board of reviewers, although some editors find reviewers for articles on specialized
topics. Such reviewers generally are experienced authors and
experts from the profession. Reviewers typically are volunteers,
too, and must work their reviewing time around other full-time
responsibilities. This fact accounts for some of the lag time between when an article is submitted and when it is published.
That time also can be extended if there is any need for the
manuscript to go out for a second round of reviews. Some journals will print both the dates of receipt and acceptance to give
you an idea of lag time.

Most reviewers try their best to be prompt, impartial, and
helpful in the review comments they develop. Caustic or totally
negative reviews seldom provide help to prospective authors and
may serve to discourage some. Reviewers usually are selected
because they have special expertise, understand what the journal
is trying to accomplish, and can be helpful to authors. Most
editors provide guidelines to reviewers as aids in their decision
making.

Some journals publish or make their review guidelines
available to interested authors. If you obtain such information,
review an early draft of your article or ask one or more colleagues to review it according to such guidelines. Keep in mind
that the guidelines for authors and those for reviewers usually
are different. Try to obtain both sets of guidelines.

Sometimes your article will be rejected simply because it

falls outside the periodical's scope or because you failed to adhere to the stylistic requirements. Remember that your article typically is reviewed by only a few people. They may have misunderstood your intent, content, or methodological decisions. So, if your article is rejected by a journal for any of these reasons, do not be too discouraged. Rejection is not pleasant, but the experience can be educational.

Use the advice provided by editors or reviewers, resubmit if encouraged to do so, and in your next cover letter, describe how you have spoken to reviewers' concerns. Your chances for acceptance will be greatly enhanced if you work with the review comments. Some journals use the same reviewers a second time, while others will solicit new reviewers. There is no guarantee that the same or new reviewers will approve a resubmitted article, but your odds have greatly improved.

If you simply disagree with the rejection decision or any reviewers' comments, try submitting it to one of the secondary journals you had selected in the prewriting stage. Be sure that the article adheres closely to the second journal's stylistic guidelines, even if considerable change in citational or referencing formats is necessary.

The submission process is not difficult and being aware of some terminology, likely procedures, and specialized requirements will make it easier. Most editors wish you success as your success helps them produce quality publications. We encourage you to use whatever information you can acquire about procedures to facilitate your publishing efforts.

EXERCISES

1. Complete a planning activity for an article in relation to one of the journals you receive, are familiar with, or in which you would like to publish. Select one or more secondary journals. Check to see if guidelines for authors are included. Do they publish a clear statement of their purpose and normal readership? Identify some of the literature areas you will need to search to establish a foundation for your article.

Develop an outline and time line for your effort. You may wish to establish additional planning activities and tie them to our earlier prewriting suggestions.

2. Select one or two types of articles that interest you (see Figure 8.1). Examine some periodicals that describe an intention to publish such types or until you find two or more articles that seem to fit the category description. Observe how the articles are formatted, including the way information is presented, citations are used, and practices followed that seem specific to the type. Over time, obtain a collection of articles that seem to emulate the various types you hope to publish.

ENDNOTE

1. *Adult Education Quarterly, Adult Learning, American Educational Research Journal, American Journal of Education, Communication Education, Comparative Education, Contemporary Educational Psychology, Educational Administration Quarterly, Educational Gerontology, Educational Leadership, Educational Psychologist, Educational Studies, Gender and Education, HRD Quarterly, International Journal of Computers in Adult Education and Training, International Journal of Educational Research, International Journal of Lifelong Education, International Journal of Qualitative Studies in Education, Journal of Educational Policy, Journal of Educational Psychology, Journal of Higher Education, Journal of Learning Disabilities, Journal of Research and Development in Education, Phi Delta Kappan, Psychology and Aging, Small Group Research, Sociology of Education, Studies in Educational Evaluation, Studies in the Education of Adults,* and *Training.*

CHAPTER 9

Maximizing the Personal Computer in Writing

We recognize that not all writers or prospective authors use personal computers or will want to use them. You may have read stories about famous authors who create manuscripts with a pencil, pen, or old mechanical typewriter in some mountaintop cabin. You may feel that such an approach fits you. Whatever works best is what you should use and you already know much about your preferences. Be aware, though, of the ways personal computers or terminals connected to mainframe computers can enhance your writing effort. This chapter describes computing features a writer can use, ways of employing computer networks for managing or accessing information, and ways of enhancing collaborative writing efforts with computers.

WORD PROCESSING

Perhaps the personal computer's biggest advantage is in its writing and revising capabilities through word processing software. Such software (a program of computer instructions) allows for easy storage and retrieval of words you have typed on a keyboard and saved. This information can be stored as a file on floppy disks or saved on a hard drive mechanism that stores material internally. Even if saving large amounts of information internally for fast access, it is always a good policy to save all your files on floppy disks as backup copies. A corresponding disadvantage of using a personal computer is relying completely on the technology. If you experience electronic or mechanical failure, you may be prevented from accessing or using the most recent version of a created text.

Once you have keyed in your text, the word processing software makes deleting, moving, rearranging, or changing material easy and rapid. Computer software lets you apply special stylistic features as desired or required by a publisher. For example, you can underline, use bold print, and italicize words.

If connected to a high quality printer, a sophisticated word processing package can help you complete a manuscript that is visually correct and attractive. It can control the margin size, type of print font, and even size of print. Many programs also facilitate the creation of impressive tables, charts, and graphic designs.

To select a word processing package that works for you, talk with colleagues, read reviews of various packages, and even try them out before purchasing or regularly using them. In making your decision, you may need to consider the package's compatibility with what colleagues or others use. You may be able to connect electronically to a large institutional mainframe computer that supports one or more of the word processing programs you prefer. In choosing or purchasing a particular software package, there are various important software features you should consider.

Outlining

Most software packages contain an outlining option, although you may wish to purchase a special outlining program. Since some publishers and journal editors require you to submit an outline before the invitation to complete an article is extended, such software can be quite useful. This function is especially useful when coauthoring an article so all coauthors have a clear idea of the entire direction for any writing effort.

As discussed in Chapter 4, outlining can be helpful in arranging, rearranging, or expanding prewriting thoughts and thinking through all possibilities for a manuscript. If you do not use outlining regularly, it might require a little time in reading and following directions or perhaps some trial and error to make the tool work for you. We encourage you to use such a feature at least once to demonstrate its prewriting potential.

Before you select a program you may wish to compare several outlining programs, seek advice from colleagues who use outlining in their writing, and read any available reviews. Here are some features of the WordPerfect® 5.1's outlining option as an example of what you might find attractive:

- It inserts outline characters (numbers and letters) automatically.
- If you need to rearrange, add to, or delete parts of an outline, WordPerfect automatically renumbers everything.
- Up to eight indented levels can be used.
- The outline can easily be edited and entire sections moved to new locations.
- Two or more independent outlines can be created in the same document.
- You can select various numbering styles, such as regular outline, paragraph, legal, and symbols (a bullet).

Figure 9.1 shows the original outline submitted to our editor as a display of the projected contents for Chapter 1.

Macros

A macro is the combination of several steps or key strokes stored internally in your computer and invoked whenever you execute a very few key strokes. It is a small computer program that you can create. Macros are very powerful because they can be used both for simple or routine procedures and for very complicated ones that require many key strokes. They can save time, simplify certain procedures, customize the software to your particular needs, and routinize those actions you will do over and over again in your writing process, such as underlining several words, italicizing certain words, and establishing or

Chapter 1:   Introduction to Writing for Publication

I.   Why should you write?
     A. Writing and the profession
     B. Informing your profession

II. Stages in the writing process
     A. The art of good writing
         1. Prewriting activities
         2. Text development
     B. Revising and editing

III. Writing blocks

IV. The publication process
     A. Why articles are accepted and rejected
     B. What editors look for

V.   Characteristics of successful writers
     A. Perseverance and self-discipline
     B. Curiosity and lifelong learning
     C. Other characteristics

VI. Writing resources
     A. Stylistic guidelines
     B. Dictionary, thesaurus, and writing guides
     C. Computer software

Figure 9.1 Original outline of the book's first chapter.

changing margins. Think of a macro as the writer's efficiency tool.

Creating macros is relatively easy with most word processing packages and normally takes only minimal understanding of the necessary programming or keystroke entry requirements. Macros can be created for both the DOS and Macintosh worlds (two different computer operating systems). In the DOS world, macros normally are created, saved in a special file, and then invoked when the user pushes special key combinations. In the

MAC world, a macro creating option is available with the normal system software. Macro file icons typically are created for subsequent clicking with a mouse to invoke them.

In WordPerfect® 5.1, for example, you simply hold down the "Ctrl" key and then hit the "F10" key. This action invokes a message at the bottom of the screen that asks you to define the macro. You then define a combination of the "Alt" key and any letter key as one of the standard "macros" you wish to create for a sequence of key strokes normally repeated time and time again in the course of your typing. This is followed by hitting the sequence of key strokes to be included in that one macro. Then you save the sequence to memory by hitting the "Ctrl" and "F10" keys simultaneously. That ends the creation of that macro and from then on, each time you hit the "Alt" and that key in combination, the longer sequence of key strokes automatically and rapidly takes place. In Wordperfect® you can also create temporary macros for a current editing session through the "variables" feature. With either technique your work is reduced and simplified.

As an illustration, the typing of "WordPerfect® 5.1" requires 24 different key stokes each time, including selecting the trademark symbol from a separate file that contains numerous special characters. A macro was defined for this book (the "Alt" key being held down at the same time the letter "W" is hit) for the 24 strokes so that each time the words and symbol are needed in a sentence, it can be accomplished in two strokes rather than 24.

The software also allows you to type in words (up to eight characters) for the definition instead of the "Alt" key and a single letter. Then when you want to invoke a macro, you simply hit the "Alt" and "F10" keys simultaneously, a message appears at the screen's bottom calling for the characters in your definition, and you type in those letters. Thus, you have an almost unlimited number of macros that can be defined. The biggest problem in creating and using macros is keeping track of what you have created.

The list of macros in Figure 9.2 illustrates some possibili-

1. Capitalize the next letter.
2. Erase the next paragraph.
3. Underline the next word.
4. Italicize the next word.
5. Build a bibliography by switching to a master file of references, allowing the author to select the appropriate citation, and then alphabetizing it within a reference section.
6. Alphabetize a set of references.
7. Print out a draft copy of a manuscript on a dot matrix printer.
8. Print out a final copy of a manuscript on a laser printer, with the option given the author for a single key stroke to indicate the number of copies desired.
9. Type out a word or several words used frequently in the manuscript, such as a publisher, specific phrase, or name. An example is: WordPerfect® 5.1.
10. Change the margins, with the option given the author as to the particular dimensions desired.
11. Type a heading in all caps and centered and then reset for normal typing and moving to the appropriate location for subsequent typing.
12. Create in a separate file a list of authors cited.
13. Create a template for selecting desired desktop publishing features.
14. Select multiple words as per the author's choice and place them in a data base being created.
15. Save a document both on the internal hard drive and on a floppy disk as a backup file.

Figure 9.2 Suggested macros.

ties. Some of them capitalize on the use of a pause feature while creating the macros to allow for one or more decisions during execution. A macro also can be "looped," where it is repeated until a particular task is completed, or "nested" within another macro so that multiple tasks can be carried out.

Advanced macro creation for complex tasks in WordPerfect® 5.1 allows for the use of variables or "if-then" functions to make decision comparisons. Most software manuals have sections that describe how macros are created. Some software packages come with several macros already defined or there are organizations that provide or sell macro designs. You also can find separate books that are devoted to creating and using advanced macros. The careful creation of macros can enhance your writing.

Footnotes, Endnotes, Indexes, and Tables of Contents

Some journals or stylistic guidelines permit the use of such features as footnotes or endnotes in articles for displaying certain kinds of information. We encourage you to ascertain the editor's preferences prior to submitting your article. Some periodicals encourage or require that important terms be described by the author for inclusion in a publication's index or list of key words. You may be asked to include a table of contents, although this requirement is usually reserved for books or monographs. Most word processing software packages include options or describe procedures for invoking these features.

The creation of footnotes or endnotes as citations or as supplemental discussion is automated in most word processing packages. With special key strokes you can create the footnote or endnote immediately wherever you are in the text. The software places and numbers the citation appropriately when printing the document. Later in a subsequent draft if you add a new footnote or endnote, most packages automatically insert it in the correct location and renumber all subsequent notations. You can usually edit footnotes or endnotes, too, subsequent to their initial creation if necessary.

Footnoting is typically handled as follows. Room at the bottom of the page is automatically saved for a footnote and the number of each one sequenced consecutively. The footnote becomes visible immediately or via a view print screen feature. All footnotes are printed out, often in a smaller print font or you can so designate a smaller print font as you create them. Endnotes are created in a similar fashion and placed at the end of the manuscript or any location you designate. Viewing them may require more effort. If you use both footnotes and endnotes in the same manuscript, most software packages will be able to keep them separate in terms of placement and enumeration. The footnote at the bottom of this page and the endnote superscripted in Chapter 8 and displayed at the end of that chapter demonstrate how WordPerfect® 5.1 handles the creation process.[1]

Indexes and tables of contents are easy to create with most word processing packages. WordPerfect® 5.1 can compile an index of major topics, subtopics, or words from the text in your manuscript as you type it. You can make a second sweep through your document after it is finished to carry out the index construction process. You can even have page numbers added if desired and the words will be alphabetized in any format that you wish to establish.

Index creation is accomplished by marking or flagging text you desire for inclusion. One or two key strokes usually complete the task or a convenient macro can be designed for it as you continue to type or search for additional words to be marked. Most software programs allow you manually to create index entries to accommodate special language or jargon.

Tables of contents are created with procedures similar to those used for developing indexes. You mark or flag the text in a special way and then you are given the opportunity to indicate the level or how it is to be indented and the location desired for the subsequent page numbers.

Other Features

Word processing packages possess many more features that you will learn to use as ways of enhancing your writing. Features such as adding headers or footers, numbering pages, being able to incorporate graphics, utilizing mathematical formulas, and creating columns or tables are examples. Some jour-

---

[1]This is a sample footnote to demonstrate how it is automatically placed, formatted, and numbered.

nals will require that you have a desktop publishing capacity and that you submit camera ready copies of figures, tables, or even whole manuscripts. Windowing or pull-down menu capabilities may be something to consider as they make your use of different features easier.

CHECKING GRAMMAR AND SPELLING

When you are actively engaged in the process of writing, we recommend that you not labor over the correct spelling of those words you are unsure of, whether or not you have typed every word correctly, and whether you have used perfect grammar. For the first draft that piece of advice works well. It can be helpful for getting your initial words and thoughts out. Then, as we have noted before, prior to submitting that final copy to a publisher, you need to polish your text and correct all errors through revising and editing efforts.

Computer software developers have provided the writer with considerable help. Many word processing packages have an option for checking the spelling against a master dictionary. If your software does not contain such a feature and you purchase a separate program, make sure it is completely compatible with the type of files you create. A word of caution on spell check programs—even the best ones have limitations so don't rely totally on one. A final read through and edit are vital.

What features in a spell check program or option should you consider? You want to be able to check the spelling of a single word. This feature comes in handy when you think you know how to spell a particular word and want to quickly check to see if it is correct or if you use a word frequently throughout the manuscript but are unsure of its spelling. WordPerfect® 5.1 contains this feature. You can also easily switch to a companion thesaurus and seek out alternative words if the one you have selected does not seem correct or is overused.

You will want a large dictionary on a disk or in the computer's memory against which your software makes word comparisons for correct spelling. Some software programs provide specialized supplemental dictionaries or allow you to create them as you work to accommodate specialized words, professional rhetoric, or proper nouns that you use repeatedly.

Computer programmers have developed grammar checking programs that can be of immense value to the beginning or experienced writer. Such programs analyze a manuscript or passage and then provide analysis of the text. Some programs will provide recommendations for making changes, describe ways to improve the writing, and even develop various readability scale scores. These programs are sometimes stand-alone software packages or they may be incorporated in some word processing programs.

As mentioned before, you should seek advice from colleagues, read any available reviews, and try out or see a demonstration of a particular package before purchasing or committing yourself to using it. Consider the number of analysis features, the type of information provided back to you, the time required to complete the analysis, and whether or not it is compatible with any word processing package you might use to create your initial manuscript.

RightWriter® 3.1 was the grammar check program used to analyze parts of this book. This stand-alone software package is completely compatible with WordPerfect® 5.1. It provides several results, such as a readability index score, a strength index which measures the strength and clarity of the writing, a descriptive index which measures how terse or wordy a manuscript might be, and a jargon index. It also provides suggestions on how to improve particular sentences, asks questions about the use of certain words or terms, and may make suggestions about the use of the passive versus active voice.

Such computerized assistance can immediately improve your writing efforts. It builds confidence to know that errors or problems you might miss as you write or edit will be caught at a later stage. Coupled with the critiques by colleagues we described in earlier chapters, a personal computer and all its many possibilities should enable you to create well-written articles.

DATA AND INFORMATION MANAGEMENT

Personal computer uses to enhance your writing capability go beyond word processing. For instance, using the computer to access and manage information can be extremely important for some writers. The amount of information you need increases and accumulates with your writing experience. You may decide to purchase software specifically designed for managing or analyzing large amounts of information.

Over time, some writers create large master bibliographies of citations used in previous writings or of potential use in future writings. The fifth macro in Figure 9.2, for example, could be used to extract references from a master bibliography and build a reference list for any manuscript being created. Any new references generated then could be added to such a bibliography to keep it current. Via WP Citation® (a reference generating software package that is a companion to WordPerfect® 5.1), such references can be available in a multitude of citational styles.

You may wish to invest in communication software that facilitates the connection of your personal computer to a mainframe computer or to an electronic network. This connection completed via an external or internal device called a modem, especially if it is high speed, permits you to access information stored in computers literally around the world, to use various software packages, and to use various printing, plotting, or graphic creation devices. For example, we can connect to various mainframe computers on our respective campuses which then provides access to a multitude of on-campus electronic data bases, university library card catalogues, and data analysis or production aids. Off campus we can connect to numerous data bases or discussion groups, electronic journals, and electronic networks.

Many advantages related to information exchange and collaboration exist once you have external connection capabilities. You can exchange text with colleagues or seek information related to your writing endeavors from others. You can collaborate at a distance by exchanging disks or sending information electronically. You can even obtain software that allows you to send information to a colleague electronically with all special characters or features intact, such as graphics, underlining, or italicizing. You also can have your initial information critiqued by others through electronic exchanges.

In a recent coauthored book project, half the chapters were word processed with WordPerfect® 5.1 on a DOS (one type of computer operating system) computer and half with Word® on a Macintosh (another type of operating system) computer. Then the chapters were saved in text files (one procedure for preparing information so it can be transferred electronically) and exchanged electronically via Bitnet, a network that connects with other networks throughout the world. From there the chapters were downloaded electronically through each author's respective mainframe computer into the different word processing package, reworked, sent back to the original author the same way, and the exchange repeated until a final draft of each chapter was accepted.

In the face of approaching deadlines, several chapters were revised in a matter of hours, even though the authors lived thousands of miles from each other. Such rapid exchange was accomplished through email (an electronic exchange of short messages) by asking and answering questions about rewriting suggestions. Then, when all chapters were completed, they were accumulated on one author's computer so that final copies submitted to the publisher were printed with WordPerfect® 5.1 software on the same printer.

You will discover other ways for maximizing the efficacy of a personal computer in your writing and manuscript preparation. Specialized graphics programs, quantitative or qualitative data analysis software, and individualized information storage techniques are only some capabilities you may discover or develop. We recommend you experiment with a computer, ask colleagues how they use it in their writing efforts, and read several journals, magazines, or books that specialize in information about personal computers. If you are like most authors, the personal computer will quickly become an invaluable tool in creating quality articles.

EXERCISES

1. Discover how your word processing software (or how a colleague's software) can be used to create macros. Then create a macro that alphabetizes a list of references. Examine the list of macros displayed in Figure 9.2 and select at least one other you can practice developing and using in your writing effort. Think of some of the repetitious procedures you go through each time in your writing efforts and attempt to develop several macros to simplify them into a few key strokes.

2. Select at least one of the features described in this chapter (such as outlining, grammar checking, or electronic information exchange) with which you are not familiar. Use your own personal computer or use one that you can access and master that feature. Practice using the feature in your next writing effort to expand your ability to maximize the potential of the personal computer.

CHAPTER 10

Strategies for Successful Writing

Successful writing is not the result of magic, mystery, or miracle. Knowledge and skill inform the process and contribute to an effective manuscript. As you write, a number of useful strategies and techniques for productive, effective, and efficient text development can help you. Throughout this book we have presented many valuable suggestions for improving your writing. In this chapter we focus on some special strategies we have developed throughout our combined years of writing and editing.

REDUCING THE LENGTH OF ARTICLES

As we described in Chapter 8, most journals limit articles in terms of maximum number of words or pages. Since competition to publish is considerable, we urge you to reduce your manuscript as much as possible while still maintaining quality and conveying your message. This economy improves your chances of a speedier publication.

We recommend you put your manuscript through what we call the tally reduction process as the last step before submission but after the editing and revising stages. This suggestion is based on an assumption that many individuals overwrite using more words than are necessary to convey essential meaning. This "tightening up" strategy usually results in eliminating unnecessary or redundant words, facilitating use of the active voice, and generally producing a better reading version of your text.

The tally reduction process includes four stages. The first step begins with simply counting or estimating the number of words in what you consider your final version (many word processing packages have a word count option).

In step two, establish a word reduction target. We suggest setting a goal of reducing 10 to 20 percent of the words in your text. Many writers, at least in the beginning stages of their writing careers, can quite easily achieve this goal. If the journal you find of interest has established an upper word limit and your article is considerably longer, establish an even higher goal. If your article contained 4,200 words and your reduction target were 15 percent, you would attempt to remove 630 words from the manuscript.

The third step is to set an average target for each page. For example, let's assume you had 16 pages of text exclusive of the references section (references normally can be reduced only by eliminating them). Then divide the 630 words by 16 and plan to remove an average 40 words per page.

Step four involves rereading a hard copy of the document page by page, eliminating redundant or unnecessary words, and keeping a tally of the number removed. Attempt to average the 40 word goal, perhaps keeping a running total as you move through the document. We recommend using the upper right hand corner of each page to record your tallies. We find that using the traditional tally marking procedure of four vertical lines with the fifth line crossing the previous four to indicate sections of five works well. Hence the name we have given this procedure. Appendix C provides some specific strategies on how to make such reductions.

You can also reduce a manuscript's length by eliminating bulky, awkward, and convoluted sentence structures. Streamlining syntax shortens the text and increases its effectiveness. Along with cutting the article by restructuring sentences you can use the active rather than the passive voice. The active voice invests your text with energy, eliminates useless verbiage, and usually cuts unnecessary and confusing constructions.

A THREE BY THREE RULE

In our workshops we describe the three by three rule. It is a mnemonic device to help beginning writers consider the possibilities before them as authors. The first "three" refers to a minimal number of possible articles related to any good idea, research project, or topic of personal interest.

Say you have just completed a research project examining the learning activities of 300 older adults. The first article could describe the basic research findings and be aimed at a research journal. Another article for either a research journal or a practitioner's magazine could provide information about gender differences in older adult learning and speculate on the implications for planning educational programs. A third article could discuss some policy implications related to involving older adults in learning efforts and be published in an educational policy journal. In essence, we suggest gleaning from your data or ideas all that you can. Then multiply your efforts by not putting everything into a single article.

The second "three" refers to the minimal number of times we recommend you attempt to have a single article published. Rejection by the first journal is not at all unusual. Competition for journal publication is steep and first-time submissions often encounter rejection. But don't give up because of a simple rejection! Most authors face many rejection letters in their careers. If you have a good idea, try it out with at least two more journals before you consider giving up on that particular article. A word of caution, though: Do not submit the same manuscript simultaneously to more than one journal.

In Chapter 8, we talked about identifying one or more secondary journals in your initial planning efforts. If you do receive an initial rejection, send the article to one of your secondary journals but ensure that it meets that periodical's appropriate stylistic requirements. This submission may mean reformatting the article but such an effort should not take much time, especially if you are using a word processor. Make the same effort at least one more time even if you receive a second rejection. Frequently, you will receive feedback from editors or reviewers in those initial rejection letters that can help you in revising the text.

COPY EDITING

Copy editing (what an editor does to a manuscript before sending it off to a typesetter) can be a tedious and time-consuming task. Most authors fail to realize how even small amounts of sloppiness, inconsistency, and inaccuracy can consume an editor's time. A typical journal article has quite a journey before it is ever published. It is not unusual that an article will be read by at least five (internal and external) reviewers, be read minimally twice and sometimes as many as four or five times by at least three of these reviewers, and then undergo a copy editing process that can take from two to eight hours depending on the initial shape of the text.

Why does a publishable article submitted by a competent author involve so much work at the copy editing stage? A manuscript that is sent to a typesetter must rigorously adhere to stylistic rules and standards because of the printer's typesetting expectations. Even keyboarders in a desktop publishing situation or when text is transmitted electronically will expect authors to follow publishing and stylistic rules consistently. Extra communication between the editor and printer or editor and author to correct problems serves to raise the cost of publication.

We urge you to do as much of your own copy editing as possible in the revising and editing stages before submitting an article. You not only speed up the process and cut down on publishing costs, you enhance the possibilities of the text being published. Following are several reasons why copy editing skills are valuable:

1. An article with many stylistic problems frequently will be returned to the author for changes before it ever enters the review process. This action obviously means a time delay and more work for the author.

2. An article that is circulated to reviewers may still receive less than glowing commentary if the reviewers feel that stylistic

problems or lack of adherence to stylistic guidelines get in the way of effective communication.

3. The author's copy editing (of a next to final draft) before submitting an article to an editor usually will result in a better finished product. You may be able to copy edit during the tally reduction process or may desire to do it with an earlier draft.

4. Learning copy editing skills and thoroughly understanding a set of stylistic guidelines, such as the APA requirements, will result in an improved text.

Appendix D portrays some standard marks to practice as you develop your copy editing skills.

Here is a summary of some problems common among manuscripts:

- Using incorrect punctuation marks or grammatical protocols
- Not adhering strictly to the stylistic guidelines
- Making sentences too long or complicated
- Using incorrect or inconsistent heading styles
- Using incorrect or inconsistent seriation marks (for example, APA requires letters rather than numbers within paragraph seriation and numbers for paragraph seriation)
- Using stylistically incorrect or inadequate citational information (for instance, some rules change when within parentheses as opposed to outside of parentheses)
- Using incorrect citational information (an incorrect date or suspected incorrect date may necessitate an editor or staff member making telephone contact with an author, carrying out some library searching activity, or searching some data base by computer)
- Using indefinite references (such as "this" or "there")
- Using inadequate transitional words or sentences at the concluding or beginning paragraphs of a section
- Overusing the word "the" (and other articles)

SOME LEGAL AND ETHICAL ISSUES

We urge prospective authors to consider various ethical and legal issues and concerns. Become informed about copyright protection. The United States copyright laws are in place to protect the intellectual property of authors. You should honor these laws. Someday they may protect your own published work. In practice it means citing correctly and appropriately the help given you by published authors. Direct quotes should be accurately referenced according to the rules established by whatever stylistic guidelines you are following. Give appropriate credit when paraphrased or summarized material or others' ideas serve as a genesis for your own thoughts. Always be attentive to appropriate acknowledgment.

Some publishers will require that you obtain written permission if you use an extensive amount of words from the same published source. Publishers and stylistic guidelines vary on this practice. The APA *Publication Manual* (1983) permits the use of up to 500 words from an APA copyrighted source without written permission; any copyright owner can exact more stringent requirements. Some publishers will require that you obtain written permission for other items (such as figures, tables, and appendixes) you use, cite, or duplicate from previously published work. Such requirements usually will be described in the author's guidelines or they may be delineated within a prescribed standard stylistic guide. Figure 7.3 (in Chapter 7) contains a generic form that can be used to obtain written permission. Some editors will give citing or quoting permission orally and use a more informal follow-up memo for confirmation.

Many periodicals require you to provide a signed warrant statement. Such statements generally cover both legal and ethical considerations. They require that you assert you are submitting original work, work not accepted by another publication, and work not being simultaneously submitted to another publication; that you are not infringing on any known copyrighted material; and that you are not including any libelous statements. Check the journal to which you are submitting your article for specific wording requirements.

As we noted earlier in this chapter, do not submit the same article to more than one periodical at the same time. It might be tempting to do so if you face great pressures to publish, but you could not honestly sign most warrant statements and would need to withdraw from one if both accepted your article. Stories do surface from time to time regarding authors who have had the same article published in two journals with dire consequences usually resulting. There could be times when you are asked if your article could be reprinted in another periodical. The permission for such a venture usually comes from the publisher unless someone else owns the copyright.

One more issue discussed here deals with a stance you may need to make regarding paying submission fees. The high cost of publication has necessitated some periodicals charging a flat fee or a fee per page to publish an article. Other journals charge such fees out of a profit motive. For some authors, being faced with paying this type of fee presents an ethical dilemma. You may face this dilemma yourself.

SOME FINAL THOUGHTS

We have provided various writing tips, strategies, and suggestions throughout this book. We conclude with a summary of several points we hope will serve as motivators to begin the publishing process.

1. In order to get an article published, you first must write one. Just getting started is the biggest stumbling block for many people. So have confidence that you can do it and develop the necessary self-discipline to carry through.

2. Study the most timely topics in the field. Articles that are unique, future-oriented, and focused on current practical issues are often ones worth writing.

3. Study the periodicals. They will provide clues to the types of topics being accepted and the required stylistic guides. Select the one that appears most suitable for the first submission of your article.

4. Target your article by figuring out what the journal and its readers want.

5. Say what you have to say as economically as possible. Consider presenting your ideas in public before putting or final-

izing them into an article so you can obtain early feedback and become clearer in what you have to say.

6. An article's lead paragraph or two are very important as they catch the reader's attention. Spend considerable time thinking about and developing them.

7. Make sure that you have good transitioning words and sentences throughout your article. Transitions are the bridges that keep your reader's interest in the article high.

8. Use the four stages of writing and get it written! Write a first draft without worrying about correctness and exact wording. Seek the opinions of others, revise, and edit.

9. Don't be too solicitous in what you have to say, nor too critical of others' work. Be professionally assertive without being obnoxious in what you do, as your published material makes you a peer with other authors in your field.

10. Submit a perfect copy to the journal, one that looks attractive, adheres to appearance requirements, and is error free.

11. Use a short, dynamic cover letter. It should be professionally written and sell the article. Point out the article's value to readers and mention that you have adhered to the journal's stylistic guidelines.

12. Discover what writing style works best for you. Learn about your writing strengths and weaknesses from your own assessment and the critique of others. Learn from any mistakes by keeping track of such assessments and avoiding errors or weaknesses the next time.

Believe in yourself as a writer. Keep writing and you can become a successful author.

EXERCISES

1. Take several pages of something you have already written. Set a high overall word reduction target of at least 25 percent and using the tally method, attempt to reach your goal. As an alternative exercise, try to accomplish that goal on each page.

2. Using the three by three rule introduced earlier, select an idea you have for a journal article and determine if you can outline at least three different manuscripts. Determine the different kinds of periodicals you may need to seek as outlets.

APPENDIX A

Removing Gender, Stereotyped, or Ethnic Bias in Professional Writing

1. The easiest way to remove a gender-specific pronoun is to convert it to the plural form.

   Poor: Above all, the adult student brings to adult education a high level of motivation. His purposes are clear and the rewards high.

   Better: Most adult students bring a high level of motivation to the adult education setting. Their purposes usually are clear and their resulting rewards high.

2. The use of "man" or "mankind" to indicate a larger or universal class of individuals can be corrected by using the term human or people.

   Poor: Thinking is another of Man's vocations.

   Better: Thinking is another human vocation.

   Poor: The grown person has many vocations: those to which he is called to earn his living and those to which he chooses as ways of enjoying life.

   Better: Mature people have many vocations: those to which they are called for earning a living and those they chose as means for enjoying life.

3. The use of "he or she," "s/he," or something like "womyn" to obtain the correct sound but avoid spelling the word with "man" in it should be avoided because of the awkwardness, lack of clarity, and extra words required.

Poor: The adult teacher often lacks formal training, al-
          though he or she might have many years of prac-
          tical experience.

Better: Adult teachers often lack formal training, although
          they may have many years of practical experience.

Poor: As a person matures, his or her self-concept moves
          from being a dependent personality to being a self-
          directed human being.

Better: As a person matures, the self-concept moves from
          being a dependent personality toward being a self-
          directed human being.

4. Avoid using words that can be perceived as derogatory or
   stereotyped.

Poor: Radicals or women's libbers are working toward
          equality.

Better: Supporters of the women's movement are working
          toward equality.

6. Avoid using words that can be perceived as ethnically or
   religiously biased.

Poor: Biblebelt fundamentalists were the main cause of
          the Republican party's presidential defeat in 1992.

Better: Differences in conservative religious views were im-
          portant among causes of the Republican party's
          presidential defeat in 1992.

APPENDIX B

Sample Cover Letter

Dear [editor's name]:

    Enclosed are three copies of an article entitled, "The Older Adult as Self-Directed Learner." I ask that it be considered for publication in [name of the journal]. I have followed your stylistic guidelines and prepared two of the copies for an anonymous review. The article has not been submitted for publication to any other journal. [Add the following if a warrant statement is required: A signed warrant statement is included with this letter.]

    You will note that the article summarizes data from a recently completed longitudinal study of older adult learners. The research stems from earlier work reported in your journal by Jones (vol. 9, pp. 72–86), Smith (vol. 10, pp. 16–30), and Adams (vol. 10, 176–188). I believe many readers of the journal will find the resulting curricular model to be useful in planning local programs for seniors.

    I will be happy to answer any questions you may have about the article. Thank you for your assistance.

Sincerely yours,

[your name and title]

(add a warrant statement if required)

APPENDIX C

Strategies for Shortening a Manuscript

1. Substitute for some of your prepositional phrases.

   Old: institutions of higher education . . .
   New: higher education institutions . . .

2. Remove some of the illustrative, cuing, or descriptive phrases.

   Old: For example, adult education as a discipline . . .
   New: Adult education as a discipline . . .
   Old: self-directed learning approaches (e.g., learning projects) . . .
   New: self-directed learning approaches . . .

3. Remove some words used to indicate a pause at the start of a sentence.

   Old: However, it is frequently the case . . .
   New: It is frequently the case . . .

4. Substitute one word for three or four.

   Old: A variety of publishing houses . . .
   New: Various publishers . . .
   Old: In the majority of the cases, higher education . . .
   New: Usually higher education . . .

5. Remove some proper nouns or prestigious titles.

   Old: Dr. Robert Jones (1981) noted that . . .
   New: Jones (1981) noted that . . .

6. Remove fun, cute, personal, needless, or catchy phrases.

   Old: In the author's opinion, instructional design . . .
   New: Instructional design . . .

7. Avoid jargon, abbreviations, and acronyms.

   Old: The instructional approach was pedagogically sound . . .
   New: A sound instructional approach . . .

8. Remove some modifying or qualifying phrases.

   Old: Research by people like Dewey and Rogers . . .
   New: Some educators' research—or—Dewey's and Rogers's research . . . (see no. 10)
   Old: Brown (1991) was somewhat reluctant to . . .
   New: Brown (1991) was reluctant to . . .

9. Remove some descriptive names that an interested reader could find if really necessary.

   Old: The Pergamon Press consortium, consisting of the U.K., the United States, Canada, and Australia, produced several . . .
   New: The Pergamon Press consortium produced several . . .

10. Use possessives to replace some words.

    Old: The sociological theory of Adams (1990) . . .
    New: Adams's (1990) sociological theory . . .

11. Use semicolons as occasional connectors rather than starting new sentences.

   Old: Gate's (1982) initial work on learning activities established a definitional base. A more extensive effort to build learning definitions was carried out by Rodriguez (1988).

   New: Gate's (1982) work on learning activities established some definitions; Rodriguez (1988) added to these.

12. Substitute fewer words with the same meaning.

   Old: some of what is known about learning . . .
   New: some aspects of learning . . .
   Old: It is obvious that social workers need . . .
   New: Obviously, social workers need . . .

13. Avoid telling people what they already know or can easily surmise.

   Old: It is known, of course, that behavioral objectives . . .
   New: [if it is known, don't state it at all]

14. Use the active rather than the passive voice.

   Old: Several million American adults are limited by being unable to read or write.
   New: Illiteracy limits several million American adults.

15. Avoid unneeded adjectives and adverbs.

   Old: Interviews took place in a large auditorium . . .
   New: Interviews took place in an auditorium . . .
   Old: Participants stared intensely at the monitor . . .
   New: Participants stared at the monitor . . .

16. Avoid unspecific or indefinite language.

    Old: Recently, the number of new undergraduates seems to be decreasing.

    New: There were fewer undergraduates this year.

17. Use positive forms of words or statements.

    Old: The subjects were not aware of the teacher.

    New: The subjects were unaware of the teacher.

18. Avoid the combination of both positive and negative comments.

    Old: The answer is not to find fault with the past theories. It is to build new theories.

    New: The answer is to build new theories.

19. Avoid overusing certain explanatory or descriptive words, such as *however, in addition, thus,* and *therefore.*

20. Cut out unnecessary evidence or anecdotes. One example is usually enough and folksy anecdotes slow down the pace.

21. Avoid using such speculative terms or phrases as *often possible, may be possible, if you wish, as it were,* and *so to speak.*

22. If the material is well written, you may need to eliminate entire sentences, whole paragraphs, complete sections, tables, and figures.

23. To help in decisions about what to remove, ask the following question: Will the meaning of this sentence or paragraph change if I remove this word or change this phrase?

APPENDIX D

Commonly Used Copy Editor's Marks

GENERAL REQUIREMENTS

Margin Marks:	Within Text Indications or Marks:	Meaning:
(stet)	Writing articles is not	Let stand as set
Au?	(Geragogy) is now known	Query to author
(sp)	State of (NY)	Spell out
∫	That is true. Usually	Start a new line
ok/?	Use the term (androgogy)	Typeset as shown

INDENTATION, POSITION, AND SPACING REQUIREMENTS

Margin Marks:	Within Text Indications or Marks:	Meaning:
¶	¶ The population was	Begin paragraph
⌣	Therefore, w e need	Close up space

Margin Marks:	Within Text Indications or Marks:	Meaning:
‖	The first report was never verified	Left justify
⌐	Adult learners	Move left
⌐ (move right bracket)	The first finding	Move right
no ¶	the study group. Therefore, it was	No paragraph
(tr)	Thier major difficulty	Transpose
(tr)	It never was known	Transpose words

INSERT OR DELETE REQUIREMENTS

Margin Marks:	Within Text Indications or Marks:	Meaning:
a/	Adult education is now	Correct marked word
℘	That there is only one	Delete marked word
⌃,	Therefore he was able	Insert comma
⌃:	Use the following	Insert colon
/=/	Self directed learning	Insert hyphen
(/)	Five point Likert scale	Insert parentheses
⊙	It was the main idea	Insert period
study ⌃	The research was	Insert shown words

SIZE OR STYLE REQUIREMENTS

Margin Marks:	Within Text Indications or Marks:	Meaning:
(bf)	Hypothesis One	Boldface type
(lc)	The Main point was	Lower case letter
(cap)	it is known that	Set in capitals
(ital)	Lifelong Learning	Set in italic
(ul)	The Research Design	Underline as shown

BIBLIOGRAPHY

REFERENCES

American Psychological Association. (1983). *Publication manual* (Third Edition). Washington, DC: The Association.

Brunk, G. G. (1989). *Social science journals: A review of research sources and publishing opportunities for political scientists.* Washington, DC: PS.

Gunning, R. (1968). *The techniques of clear writing* (Rev. Ed.). New York: McGraw-Hill.

Hubbard, J. T. W. (1989). *Magazine editing for professionals.* Syracuse, NY: Syracuse University Press.

Marquis Academic Media. (1981). *Directory of publishing opportunities in journals and periodicals* (5th Edition). Chicago: Marquis Academic Media.

Mullins, C. J. (1977). *A guide to writing and publishing in the social and behavioral sciences.* New York: Wiley. [Reprinted by Robert E. Krieger Publishers, Malabar, FL, 1983]

Office of Research and Evaluation in Adult and Continuing Education. (1989). *RE/ACE journal index for adult and continuing education research.* DeKalb, IL.: Office of Research and Evaluation in Adult and Continuing Education, Northern Illinois University.

Progoff, I. (1975). *At a journal workshop: The basic text and guide for using the intensive journal.* New York: Dialogue House Library.

Strunk, W., Jr., & White, E. B. (1979). *The elements of style* (3rd ed.). New York: Macmillan.

University of Chicago Press. (1982). *The Chicago manual of style: For authors, editors, and copywriters* (13th Ed., revised and expanded). Chicago: University of Chicago Press.

SUGGESTED READINGS

Guides to Effective Writing

Apps, J. W. (1982). *Improving your writing skills: A learning plan for adults.* Chicago: Follett Publishing Company.

Becker, H. S. (1986). *Writing for social scientists: How to start and finish your thesis, book or article.* Chicago: University of Chicago Press.

Bennett, J. (1980). Getting your manuscript into print. *English Journal, 69(7),* 31–34.

Berry, R. (1986). *How to write a research paper.* Oxford: Pergamon Press.

Boston, B. (1986). *Stet!: Tricks of the trade for writers and editors.* Alexandria, VA: Editorial Experts.

Brockett, R. G. (1985). Tips for the practitioner on writing book reviews. *Lifelong learning: An omnibus of practice and research,* 8(5), 29–31.

Carter, S. (1987). *Writing for your peers.* New York: Praeger Books.

Cook, C. K. (1985). *Line by line: How to improve your own writing.* Boston: Houghton Mifflin.

Day, R. A. (1989). *How to write and publish a scientific paper.* Cambridge: Cambridge University Press.

Dowling, L., & Evanson, J. (1990). *Writing articles: A guide to publishing in your profession.* Dubuque, IA: Kendall/Hunt Publishing Company.

Elbow, P. (1973). *Writing without teachers.* London: Oxford University Press.

Elbow, P. (1981). *Writing with power: Techniques for mastering the writing process.* New York: Oxford University Press.

Flesch, R. F., & Lass, A. H. (1982). *A new guide to better writing.* New York: Warner Books.

Fontaine, A., & Glavin, W. A., Jr. (1987). *The art of writing nonfiction.* Syracuse, NY: Syracuse University Press.

Forman, J. (1992). *New visions of collaborative writing.* Portsmouth, NH: Heinemann Educational Books, Inc.

Franklin, S., & Madian, J. (Eds.). (1987). *The writing notebook: Creative word processing in the classroom.* Eugene, OR: Creative Word Processing in the Classroom, 2676 Emerald.

Fulwiler, T. (Ed.). (1987). *The journal book*. Portsmouth, NH: Heinemann Educational Books, Inc., & Boynton/Cook.

Graves, D. H., & Sunstein, B. S. (Eds.). (1992). *Portfolio portraits*. Portsmouth, NH: Heinemann Educational Books, Inc.

Griffin, C. W. (1982). *Teaching writing in all disciplines*. London: Jossey Bass.

Gunning, R., & Mueller, D. (1963). *How to take the fog out of writing*. Chicago: The Dartnell Corporation.

Henson, K. T. (1988). Writing for education journals. *Phi Delta Kappan, 69,* 752–754.

Henson, K. T. (1993). Writing for successful publication: Advice from editors. *Phi Delta Kappan, 74,* 799–802.

Huth, E. J. (1982). *How to write and publish papers in the medical sciences*. Philadelphia: ISI Press.

Jolliffe, D. A. (Ed.). (1988). *Advances in writing research, volume two: Writing in academic disciplines*. Norwood, NJ: Ablex Publishing Corporation.

McLaughlin, G. W. (Ed.). (1985). *Effective writing: Go tell it on the mountain*. Richmond, VA: Association for Institutional Research.

Miller, C., & Swift, K. (1980). *The handbook of nonsexist writing*. New York: Lippincott & Crowell.

Millward, C., & Flick, J. (1985). *Handbook for writers*. Toronto: Hold, Rinehart and Winston of Canada.

Mirin, S. K. (1981). *Nurse's guide to writing for publication*. Wakefield, MA: Nursing Resources.

Murray, D. M. (1990). *Shoptalk: Learning to write with writers*. Portsmouth, NH: Heinemann Educational Books, Inc., & Boynton/Cook.

Murray, D. M. (1992). *What a writer needs*. Portsmouth, NH: Heinemann Educational Books, Inc.

Nerone, B. J. (1987). Preparing students to write for publication. *Nurse Educator, 12(2),* 34–35.

Noble, K. A. (1989). Good writing: What role for the educator? *British Journal of Educational Technology, 20(2),* 142–144.

Noble, K. A. (1989). Publish or perish: What 23 journal editors have to say. *Studies in Higher Education, 14,* 142–144.

Ross, S. M., & Morrison, G. R. (1993). How to get research articles published in professional journals. *Tech Trends, 38,* 29–33.

Ryckman, W. G. (1980). *What do you mean by that? The art of speaking and waiting clearly*. Homewood, IL: Dow Jones-Irwin.

Shaw, F. W. (1980). *Thirty ways to help you write*. New York: Bantam Books.

Shew, P., & Pincar, D. (1980). *Writing skills* (2nd Ed.). New York: McGraw-Hill.

Shulman, J. J. (1980). *How to get published in business/professional journals*. New York: Amacom.

Silverman, R. J. (1982). Journal manuscripts in higher education: A framework. *Review of Higher Education, 5*, 181–196.

Silverman, R. J. (1982). *Getting published in education journals*. Springfield, IL: Charles C. Thomas.

Van Til, W. (1986). *Writing for professional publication* (2nd Ed.). Newton, MS: Allyn and Bacon, Inc.

Wells, G. (1981). *The successful author's handbook*. London: Macmillan Press.

Zebrowski, E., Jr., & Werner, K. (1984). Publishing without perishing: Advice for prospective textbook authors. *Teaching English in the Two-Year College, 11(1)*, 52–60.

Zinsser, W. (1976). *On waiting well: An informal guide to writing nonfiction*. New York: Harper and Row.

Zinsser, W. (1988). *Writing to learn: How to write and think clearly about any subject at all*. New York: Harper and Row.

Guides for Finding Pertinent Periodicals

Gale directory of publications. Detroit: Gale Research.

The magazine index. Belmont, CA: Information Access Corporation.

Readers' guide to periodical literature. New York: H. W. Wilson Company.

Social science index. New York: H. W. Wilson Company.

Standard periodical directory. New York: Oxbridge Communications.

Ulrich's international periodical directory. New York: R. R. Bowker.

Ulrich's update (supplement to *Ulrich's international periodical directory*). New York: R. R. Bowker.

World media handbook. New York: United Nations Department of Public Information.

INDEX